Lafayette
AND THE
American
Revolution

Gilbert du Motier, marquis de Lafayette. From a 1792 painting by Joseph-Désiré Court.

Lafayette

AND THE

American Revolution

RUSSELL FREEDMAN

SCHOLASTIC INC.
New York Toronto London Auckland
Sydney Mexico City New Delhi Hong Kong

To Marina

ISBN 978-0-545-41647-4

Copyright © 2010 by Russell Freedman. All rights reserved.
Published by Scholastic Inc., 557 Broadway, New York, NY 10012, by
arrangement with Holiday House, Inc. SCHOLASTIC and associated
logos are trademarks and/or registered trademarks of Scholastic Inc.

12 11 10 9 8 7 6 5 4 3 2 1   11 12 13 14 15 16/0

Printed in the U.S.A.   08

First Scholastic printing, October 2011

The text typeface is Garamond #3.

Contents

View of Paris from the village of Chaillot.

⚜ ONE ⚜

The Mysterious Stranger

ON THE MORNING OF March 13, 1777, a stranger appeared in the village of Chaillot on the outskirts of Paris. He moved quietly into a gardener's house and stayed there for the next three days. No one knew who he was, where he had come from, or what he was doing in Chaillot.

The gardener was no help. He refused to talk about his guest, saying only that he was a gentleman who wished to remain anonymous. Aside from that, the gardener simply shrugged his shoulders and called his guest "the gentleman on the first floor."

While the stranger was not seen to leave the house, the neighbors noticed that he received visitors. One evening, two men on horseback rode into Chaillot, dismounted in front of the gardener's house, and slipped inside. Wrapped in dark cloaks, they had the air of men who feared they were being followed.

As the neighbors peered through their windows, a hushed and hurried conference was taking place in the house. One of the participants was an American, a representative of the colonial rebels who at that moment were fighting their War of Independence against England. Another was a French army officer, an associate of a powerful behind-the-scenes figure in French politics. The third was a nineteen-year-old nobleman named Gilbert de Lafayette; he was the gentleman on the first floor.

Lafayette hardly looked like the hero of a cloak-and-dagger mystery. Tall and spindly, he had an unusually high forehead, a long, pointed nose, and an uncertain chin. His face was freckled, and his reddish hair was powdered in the style of the French royal court. While he did not present a dashing appearance, he had other assets. He belonged to an influential aristocratic family, and he possessed an huge personal fortune. Now he was about to stake everything on the first great adventure of his life. He was planning to sail across the Atlantic and join the American revolutionaries in their battle for liberty.

There was just one big obstacle. Before he could depart for America, he had to escape from France. France was not directly involved in America's Revolutionary War, and the French government wasn't prepared to jeopardize its neutrality. For this reason, the king had forbidden French subjects to go to the aid of the colonists. To complicate matters, Lafayette, at nineteen, was a minor under French law. His legal guardian disapproved of the American rebels; he had ordered the young nobleman to mind his own business and stay in France.

Yet Lafayette had resolved to defy family and king. All his life he had dreamed of winning glory in battle and upholding his family's proud military tradition. Despite opposition, he planned to sail to America with a small group of fellow volunteers. The secret meeting in Chaillot, where he was hiding out, climaxed months of cautious preparations.

At noon on March 16, Lafayette left Chaillot as unexpectedly as he had arrived. Neighbors saw him climb into a waiting carriage and speed away in the direction of Paris.

As he passed through Paris on his way south to join the ship that would take him to America, he paused long enough to send a letter to his father-in-law, the duc d'Ayen.

The signature of the marquis de Lafayette.

"You will be astonished, my dear Papa, by what I am about to tell you," he wrote. "But I had given my word, and you would not have respected me if I had gone back on it. . . . I have found a unique opportunity to distinguish myself, and to learn my [soldier's] profession. I am a general officer in the army of the United States of America. My zeal for their cause and my sincerity have won their confidence. . . . I am overjoyed at having found such a fine opportunity to do something and to improve myself. . . . I hope to return more worthy of all who will have the goodness to miss me." He had never set foot on a battlefield, but he was off to play a crucial role in the creation of the United States of America.

✤ Two ✤

The Little Lord of Chavaniac

AS LONG AS ANYONE COULD REMEMBER, the men in Lafayette's family had ridden off to war, their fine horses prancing and snorting, the family banner flapping in the breeze. Gilbert de Lafayette was the last of his line, and as a child he heard the stories of his gallant ancestors again and again.

His father, a colonel in the French grenadiers, had been killed by an English cannon during the Seven Years' War. Three centuries earlier, another Lafayette had fought the English as a companion-in-arms of Joan of Arc.

Gilbert never knew his father. When he was born on September 6, 1757, Colonel Lafayette was away at war. The colonel never returned. Gilbert was barely two years old when he inherited the family titles and became Seigneur Marie-Joseph-Paul-Yves-Roch-Gilbert du Motier, marquis de Lafayette, baron de Vissac, and feudal lord of Chavaniac, St. Romain, Fix, and numerous other places.

After Colonel Lafayette's death, Gilbert's mother moved to Paris to play an active role in the life of the royal court. Madame Lafayette thought it essential to start forming the connections her son would need when he was ready to take his own place at court. She returned home only during summers, at the end of each Paris social season. Gilbert was left in the care of his grandmother, his two aunts, and his private tutor.

Château de Chavaniac, Lafayette's birthplace and childhood home.

He spent a lonely childhood in the family's fortress-like château, perched on a hill overlooking the red tile roofs of Chavaniac, a village of a few hundred inhabitants. His only friend and playmate was a girl, his cousin Marie, who was a year older. It wasn't possible to make friends with the village children. Gilbert, after all, was the feudal lord of Chavaniac, the ranking nobleman for miles around, and peasant children kept a respectful distance. When he walked through the village, the boys silently lifted their hats to him and the girls curtsied. Their elders did the same.

Chavaniac was a quiet place, hidden in the hills of the remote province of Auvergne, several days' ride from Paris by horse and carriage along dusty, bumpy roads. The Lafayette chateau, a massive stone building flanked on both sides by towers, had so many rooms that Gilbert wasn't sure which was the one he had been born in. In many of those rooms, his worthy ancestors gazed down at him from dark oil paintings.

Gilbert was eight years old during the winter of 1765, when a fearsome beast came out of the forest of Gévaudan, killed cattle, attacked people, and even, it was rumored, ran off with little children. It was a huge, savage, and terrible creature, people said, and as the winter wore on, it grew larger and more frightening in the minds of the villagers and became known as the "Beast of Gévaudan." Famous hunters came to bag it. The king sent his most experienced gamekeepers after it. But the animal eluded all its pursuers.

As lord of Chavaniac, Gilbert looked upon the beast as his personal foe. He imagined himself coming across the animal during one of his walks. He would attack it with his bare hands and drag it back to the village by its tail, proving himself a worthy descendant of his illustrious ancestors. "My heart pounded when I heard of [the beast]," he recalled, "and the hope of meeting it made my walks very exciting." Fortunately, that hope was never realized. The beast was finally killed by one of the king's hunters. It turned out to be nothing more than a big wolf.

Gilbert was eleven when his mother returned from Paris and told him he was now old enough to join her in the capital and begin his education as a gentleman. On the morning they departed, he climbed into the coach beside his mother and stared out the window as they drove slowly down the hill and through the village. The people of Chavaniac had lined both sides of the road to bid adieu to their little lord.

Instead of being the reigning lord for miles around, in Paris Gilbert was just a shy country boy, scarcely prepared for the sleek sophistication of the capital. Though he would someday inherit a fortune, his prospects of wealth came from his mother's side of the family, not his father's; some members of the court looked down on him as the son of a minor backwoods nobleman.

In this eighteenth-century French illustration, a woman defends herself against the "Beast of Gévaudan."

His mother enrolled him in the Collège du Plessis, a fashionable boarding school for young aristocrats. Gilbert shed his country clothes for the embroidered coats, silk stockings, and buckled shoes worn by his classmates. His sandy red hair was powdered. A small sword dangled at his side as a mark of rank.

A teacher, Monsieur René Binet, would remember him as a quiet youngster, but a boy with flashes of spirit. When his class was assigned to write an essay on the perfect horse, the teacher had in mind a disciplined animal that obeyed instantly at the sight of the rider's whip. Gilbert described the perfect horse as one that, when threatened with a whip, threw its rider and galloped off.

Once, when he felt that a classmate had been unjustly punished, Gilbert tried to raise a rebellion among his fellow students. But he didn't receive much support, and the rebellion failed. His classmates told him they agreed with him, but they were afraid to join him.

In April 1770, Gilbert's mother became very ill and died, not yet thirty-three years of age. Her father died of grief a few weeks later, leaving a vast fortune to the heartbroken boy, who came under the guardianship of his great-grandfather the comte de la Rivière. Not yet thirteen, Gilbert now was richer than any of the boys he knew, even though some ranked above him according to the strict hierarchy of the French royal court.

His great-grandfather was a proud aristocrat of the old school, a lieutenant general in the king's armies and a holder of the Grand Cross of the Royal and Military Order of St. Louis, an exceptional military honor awarded by the king. The comte de la Rivière decided that it was time for Gilbert to begin his own military career, and he obtained for the boy a commission as a cadet in the king's Black Musketeers, so called because of their sleek black horses. This was the elite corps later immortalized by Alexandre Dumas in *The Three Musketeers*.

At the same time, Gilbert was enrolled at the Academy of Versailles, the most exclusive military school in France. One of his classmates was the comte d'Artois, the king's

Lafayette at age fourteen.

grandson and himself a future king. The boys studied military tactics and took lessons in fencing, dancing, and horsemanship. Gilbert was rich enough to afford a fine string of horses, but he wasn't a particularly good rider. Tall and gangly and growing fast, he usually lost at tennis. His dancing left much to be desired.

Now that Gilbert's military career was launched, his great-grandfather began looking around for a suitable wife for him. By custom, marriages were arranged as economic and social alliances between aristocratic families. Romance was not a consideration. Gilbert's guardian set his sights on one of the most illustrious and powerful families in France. He approached the duc d'Ayen about a match between young Lafayette and the duc's second daughter, Adrienne.

At first, the duc was not enthusiastic, since his family outranked the Lafayettes. But as the comte de la Rivière pointed out, Gilbert was one of France's wealthiest young men. The duc considered this. He also considered that he had five daughters, and marriage to an acceptable nobleman would have to be arranged for each and every one of them. After giving the matter further thought, the duc agreed. Gilbert would marry Adrienne.

The next step was to draw up a marriage contract. Each family was required to give a full accounting of its assets and agree on a dowry. The delicate negotiations dragged on for months, with dozens of attorneys and family representatives taking part. Then Adrienne's mother complained that her daughter was too young to marry right away. The marriage was put off for a year, giving Gilbert time to finish his education and the young couple a chance to get acquainted. Gilbert and his bride-to-be saw each other only when Adrienne's mother was present, or when Adrienne was out for a walk with a companion.

Adrienne was already infatuated with the lanky boy in his dashing Black Musketeer's uniform, and Gilbert felt attracted to the quiet girl who seemed to understand his own lonely moods. Their wedding on April 11, 1774, was one of the great events of the Paris season. Gilbert was sixteen and a half. Adrienne was fourteen.

Lafayette's father-in-law used his influence at court to advance Gilbert's military career. Gilbert was commissioned a lieutenant in the Noailles Dragoons, a cavalry regiment under the hereditary patronage of his wife's family. He was promised a captain's commission on his eighteenth birthday. Eventually he could look forward to assuming command of the Noailles Dragoons. Someday he would have a chance to prove his worth as a soldier.

The newlyweds were expected to join in the social life of the royal court at Versailles, and they soon met everyone at court who was

Fourteen-year-old Adrienne de Noailles at the time of her marriage to sixteen-year-old Gilbert de Lafayette.

King Louis XVI of France and his queen, Marie Antoinette.

worth knowing. France had a new king, Louis XVI; his beautiful young queen, Marie Antoinette, loved to dance, play cards, and amuse herself. Lafayette never felt entirely at ease among the fashionable young noblemen and noblewomen who clustered around the queen, and his air of quiet reserve earned him a reputation for aloofness. Some of his companions felt that he was constantly brooding.

"Lafayette always seemed distant . . . with a cold, solemn look—as if he were timid or embarrassed," wrote the comte de Ségur, a school friend from the Academy of Versailles. "He was very tall and broad-shouldered, but seemed awkward, danced badly, and spoke little."

At a gala ball one evening, Lafayette was accorded the great honor of being chosen as Marie Antoinette's partner in a quadrille, a popular dance of the time. He was so clumsy that the queen stepped back and laughed at him, and the courtesans around her joined in the merriment—a humiliating episode that left Lafayette with a lasting distaste for court life.

"My awkward manner made it impossible for me to bend to the graces of the court," he later recalled.

Gilbert's attitude did not please his father-in-law. The duc obtained an appointment for Lafayette to the house of the comte de Provence, a brother of the king. Most court-iers would have welcomed this appointment as an enviable honor, but Gilbert wanted no part of it. He did not want to become a royal attendent, a servant, actually, at the expense of his military career. He couldn't simply refuse to accept the appointment, however. That would be a serious breach of court etiquette. So he managed to sabotage the appointment. At a masked ball one evening when Provence began to show off his memory, Lafayette interrupted him, saying, "Everyone knows that memory is a fool's substitute for wit."

*A masked ball at the
opera house in Paris.*

When the two men met a few days later, Provence asked Lafayette if he had known to whom he was speaking at the masked ball. "Yes," Lafayette replied, "he who wore the mask now wears a green coat." That did it. The comte turned his back on Lafayette and walked away. The appointment was withdrawn.

At court, Lafayette's behavior toward Provence was regarded as tactless and ill-mannered. But he was proud of his moment of defiance. By offending the king's brother, he had rejected any chance of pursuing a courtier's career. Now he could concentrate on his one true calling.

For a time, he was content. He took part in his regiment's summer maneuvers, enjoying the comradeship of his fellow officers and their carousing in the garrison town of Metz. While few people at court admired him, he was popular with the men of his regiment. On his eighteenth birthday, he received his captain's commission. Three months later, Adrienne presented him with their first child, a girl named Henriette.

Then his budding military career was abruptly cut short. France had been at peace for more than a decade, and a new minister of war had embarked on a strict program of reform. Entire units were demobilized. Long lists of officers were removed from active duty. One of the first to be swept aside was the newly commissioned Captain Lafayette. He had no battle experience, and his commission was solely the result of family influence. Though he retained the privileges of his rank, it might be years before he could return to active duty.

Meanwhile, he would have to put up with the life of a hanger-on at the court where he felt frustrated and out of place.

✦ THREE ✦

Why Not?

LAFAYETTE ALWAYS SAID that the turning point in his life came at a dinner he attended in 1775, when he was on summer maneuvers with his regiment at Metz. The dinner was given by his commanding general, Charles-François, the comte de Broglie, in honor of a distinguished guest, the duke of Gloucester, the younger brother of England's King George III.

Earlier that year, the long-standing quarrel between England and its American colonies had exploded into open rebellion. In April, British troops had exchanged shots with the colonists at Concord and Lexington, Massachusetts. In June, the Continental Congress had appointed George Washington commander in chief of the insurgent army. By the evening of August 8, 1775, while Lafayette and his fellow officers were dining with the duke of Gloucester, thousands of British troops were trapped in the city of Boston, which had been blockaded by Washington's rebels.

Lafayette listened with interest as Gloucester spoke of his admiration

Lafayette at eighteen in his captain's uniform of the Noailles regiment. From a painting by Louis-Léopold Boilly.

American minutemen rush off to fight the British at Concord, Massachusetts, April 19, 1775. From a nineteenth-century drawing by Felix O. L. Darley.

for the Americans and his sympathy for their cause. His brother, King George, should stop the fighting at once, he argued. He should give the Americans their independence. The rebels were fighting for their rights, said the duke, and for the rights of all mankind.

"When I first heard of [the colonists'] quarrel, my heart was enlisted," Lafayette recalled in his memoirs, "and I thought only of joining my colors to those of the revolutionaries."

The rebellion of the American colonists had excited much sympathy in France. Was it possible that the underdog Americans with their ragtag militia army could actually twist the tail of the mighty British lion?

Although France, like other European states, was an absolute monarchy, ideas of liberty and equality were in the air, inspired by a new generation of philosophers who challenged the divine right of kings, called for popular rule, and proclaimed the rights of man. The English writer John Locke argued that people are born with certain natural rights and that governments should be run for the benefit of everyone, not just of their rulers—ideas that influenced the American colonists' Declaration of Independence. And the French philosopher Voltaire (François Marie Arouet, 1694–1778) proclaimed in his 1756 *Essay on Manners*, "All men have equal rights to liberty, to their property, and to the protection of the laws".

France and England had long been rivals, and at times enemies. France had never forgiven its humiliating loss of Canada to England in the Seven Years' War. What is popularly called the French and Indian War in North America was a part of that larger conflict, and the French government watched for a chance to undermine Britain's far-flung empire. The rebellion by the American colonies offered just such an opportunity, but France could not side openly with the Americans. At the moment, France and England were at peace. The French government was not prepared to risk war on behalf of an untried little nation halfway around the world.

The American rebels wanted to establish ties with friendly governments. In July 1776, an American named Silas Deane arrived in Paris. His goal was to gain French aid and support. He found that the French government was willing to help the rebels—but only in secret.

Deane was seeking financial help, arms, equipment, and a possible alliance. And

The French philosopher Voltaire at his desk, pen in hand.

since the new American army needed experienced officers, he began to recruit French volunteers to join the American cause. French officials knew of his activities but looked the other way. Deane met potential recruits with the help of a few influential men in Paris. To encourage volunteers, he offered better pay and higher ranks than recruits could obtain in the French army. The recent French army reforms had left many career officers on indefinite reserve, without troops to command or campaigns to wage. Disgruntled by the army's reforms, and seeking some military adventure in which to distinguish themselves, ambitious officers flocked to meet Deane. By the end of 1776, he reported to Congress that he was "well-nigh harassed to death with applications of officers to go to America."

When Lafayette heard that French officers were volunteering to fight in America, he made up his mind that he wanted to go, too. So far, he had depended on his wife's family for advancement; here was a chance to accomplish something entirely on his own—an opportunity to seek glory across the Atlantic.

He discussed his plan with two close friends: his brother-in-law the vicomte de Noailles, and the comte de Ségur. The American Revolution had become a popular topic in Paris cafés, and the three young noblemen talked enthusiastically about going to America together. Above all, it would be a great adventure. Since they were all minors, they agreed to ask the consent of their families and the proper military authorities. Meanwhile they would keep their plans a secret.

Lafayette sought the advice of his former commander at Metz, the comte de Broglie, who supported the American cause and had sent a number of volunteers to Silas Deane. Broglie was not eager to help. "I watched your uncle die [in battle] in Italy," he told Lafayette. "I was commander in chief when your father was killed at Minden. In my opinion, your first duty is to your family. . . . I will have nothing to do with jeopardizing your life unnecessarily."

Lafayette would not be discouraged. When his father-in-law curtly refused to help him get permission to fight in America—"I'll make no such request for you!" the duc d'Ayen shouted—Lafayette angrily went back to Broglie. This time he met quite a different response. Broglie realized that Lafayette's wealth and family connections could prove useful to the American cause. "Good," he told the resentful young man. "Get even! Be the first to go to America! I shall take care of it!"

Broglie introduced Lafayette to one of his most trusted officers, baron de Kalb, a professional soldier who had served under Broglie in two wars. Kalb had traveled to America, where he gained a respect for the colonists and their spirit of independence. He spoke fluent English. And he had already been accepted as a volunteer officer in the American army. Impressed by the baron's distinguished military record, Deane had offered him a commission as a major general, a rank second only to that of Washington himself. In return, Kalb had promised to recruit a group of volunteer officers to sail to America under his personal leadership. He agreed to introduce Lafayette to Deane.

Deane was taken aback when he first met this nineteen-year-old boy who had never fired a shot in battle. But as he talked to the hopeful recruit, he

Baron Johann de Kalb (center) introduces Lafayette (left) to the American envoy Silas Deane. From a nineteenth-century engraving by Alonzo Chappel.

was impressed by the young man's enthusiasm and by his high birth and titles. Lafayette was the first prominent aristocrat to volunteer. No one paid attention when an obscure soldier-adventurer went off to fight in a foreign war, but if a nobleman attached to the court sailed for America, all France would sit up and take notice.

Lafayette believed that he could get his family's consent if he were given a general's rank in the American army. That's what he told Deane. He asked for a commission as a major general, the same rank granted to baron de Kalb.

Deane hesitated. He had been instructed to award ranks on the basis of a volunteer's previous service. And yet, unlike other volunteers, Lafayette was not asking for payment of any kind. He offered to serve without pay. He expected no reward other than high rank and the prospect of glory.

Deane promised the commission. When the contract was drawn up on December 7, 1776, he went to great pains to explain to the Continental Congress why he had granted the inexperienced nineteen-year-old marquis such an extraordinary honor.

He emphasized that Lafayette's family would not agree to his crossing the sea and serving in a foreign country "till he can go as a general officer." And he wrote: "The desire which the marquis de Lafayette shows of serving among the troops of the United States of North America, and the interest which he takes in the justice of their cause, make him wish to distinguish himself in this war, and to render himself as useful as he possibly can. . . . His high birth, his alliances, the great dignities which his family holds at this Court, his considerable estates in this realm, his personal merit, his reputation . . . and, above all, his zeal for the liberty of our provinces, are such as have only been able to engage me to promise him the rank of major general."

Before Lafayette could inform his family, the British ambassador in Paris issued a strong protest about the French volunteers who were sailing openly for America. To make a greater show of neutrality, French officials prohibited further crossings. The police were ordered to arrest "with plenty of publicity and severity" any French soldier who claimed to have been ordered to America by the government. Port authorities at Le Havre, an important seaport, were instructed to prevent volunteers from departing. It was widely understood that these orders were a formality. At the time, France was secretly sending arms, clothing, and equipment to the Americans. French volunteers would just have to leave more quietly in the future, so they could escape the notice of the British ambassador.

Lafayette worried that his father-in-law would use the new government policy as an excuse to put an end to his plans—despite his major general's commission. For the time being, he decided to say nothing to his family. Besides, he had thought of an excellent way to spend some of his fortune.

He went back to see Silas Deane. "Before this," he said, "you have seen only my enthusiasm; perhaps it will now become useful. I shall buy a ship to transport your officers. Be confident. I want to share your fortune in this time of danger."

Lafayette had already dispatched an agent to the seaport of Bordeaux to search for a suitable vessel. He was so elated by the prospect of sailing to America aboard his own ship that he decided to add to his family's coat of arms a defiant new motto: *Cur non?* (Why not?)

The agent sent word that he had found a sturdy merchant ship that had already made several voyages across the Atlantic.

The captain of a French merchant ship, moored just offshore, supervises the loading of cargo. From an eighteenth-century illustration.

But she needed a good overhauling before making another voyage and would not be ready to sail for several weeks. Lafayette authorized the purchase and hopefully named the ship *La Victoire*.

To deflect any suspicions about his plans, Lafayette decided to visit London, where his wife's uncle served as French ambassador. Surely no one would suspect that he was planning to fight England while he was enjoying a London vacation. Baron de Kalb was to notify him there when work on *La Victoire* was completed.

During his "vacation," Lafayette dutifully accompanied his uncle the ambassador to a succession of banquets, entertainments, and official functions. He was even presented to King George III at the British court. Though he didn't speak a word of English, he pretended to be enjoying himself. Meanwhile, he could think of nothing but *La Victoire*, sitting in dry dock in Bordeaux.

Finally, Kalb's messenger arrived in London with word that work on *La Victoire* was nearly completed. Lafayette sailed exultantly back across the English Channel. Landing in France, he hired a coach and proceeded to the village of Chaillot on the outskirts of Paris. The baron had arranged for him to hide out in a gardener's house for the next few days.

❦ FOUR ❦

Escape from France

WHILE LAFAYETTE REMAINED IN HIDING at Chaillot, baron de Kalb and William Carmichael, Silas Deane's secretary, visited him to make the final plans for the voyage. Thirteen French volunteers were to sail with him aboard *La Victoire*. They were to join the ship in Bordeaux as quickly and discreetly as possible. Deane had supplied all members of the party with letters of introduction to Congress.

Before daybreak on the morning of March 16, Lafayette slipped out of the gardener's house and rode into Paris, just minutes away. He could not resist boasting to his friends Noailles and Ségur, who had surrendered to family objections and given up their plan to fight in America. They could be trusted to keep his secret.

Lafayette burst into Ségur's room at around 7 A.M. He shut the door, sat beside his friend's bed, and told him how he had bought *La Victoire* and was about to sail to America. Leaving the amazed and envious Ségur still sitting in bed, Lafayette rushed off to break the news to Noailles. Then he galloped back to Chaillot, met Kalb, and at noon the two men set off for Bordeaux in a carriage.

As they passed through Paris, they paused long enough for Lafayette to send the

Baron de Kalb and William Carmichael, Silas Deane's secretary, met with Lafayette at his hideout in Chaillot. Kalb later sailed to America with Lafayette, served under George Washington as a major general, fought heroically, and was killed at the Battle of Camden in 1780. DeKalb, Illlinois, among other places, is named for him.

letter he had written to his father-in-law, who thought that Gilbert was still enjoying his holiday in London. Lafayette also sent a hastily written note to Adrienne, who was expecting their second child. He had told his wife nothing of his plans, and now he could not face an emotional parting scene.

"Do not be angry with me," he wrote. "Believe that I am sorely distressed. I had never realized how much I loved you—but I shall return soon, as soon as my obligations are fulfilled. Goodbye, goodbye, write to me often, every day. . . . It is terribly hard for me to tear myself away from here, and I do not have the courage to speak to you."

Lafayette and Kalb were well on their way to Bordeaux when the duc d'Ayen opened his "my dear Papa" letter from Lafayette. He was furious. No son-in-law of his was going to abandon wife and family and run off to a war that was none of France's business! As the duc raged through the house, Adrienne, devoted to her husband and comforted by her mother, hid her tears. She did her best to defend Gilbert. "I shall return soon," he had promised, and Adrienne was prepared to wait.

Her father could not be calmed. He stormed off to the Foreign Office and demanded that the king's ministers put an end to Lafayette's wild escapade. The ministers were alarmed when they heard the news. All along, they had looked the other way when volunteers sailed for America. But Lafayette was no ordinary volunteer. As a prominent nobleman and a member of the royal court, he was formally responsible to the king's ministers. His departure for America would embarrass the French government. And it would compromise France's ambassador in London, who just a few days earlier had introduced Lafayette, his nephew, to Britain's King George.

"I was extremely shocked to learn that M. de la Fayette had left for America," the ambassador complained. "Fortunately his age may excuse his thoughtlessness. This is the only consolation left to me in the chagrin I feel for so inconsiderate an action. . . . He concealed his intentions from his traveling companion, from me, and from everybody."

The French Foreign Office issued a formal order, to be approved and signed by the king: "You are forbidden to go to the American continent, under penalty of disobedience, and enjoined to go to Marseilles to await further orders." Lafayette must abandon his expedition. Instead, he was told, he must join his father-in-law and other family members in Marseilles and accompany them on an extended tour of Italy.

Lafayette and Kalb, meanwhile, had reached Bordeaux, where they planned to stay until the other members of their party arrived. As they waited, Lafayette received an urgent message from the vicomte de Loigney, a friend in Paris, describing the duc d'Ayen's angry meeting with the king's ministers and warning that a government courier was about to leave Paris with the king's order forbidding Lafayette's departure.

Lafayette had not yet received the king's order. Perhaps there was no such order. Suppose it was merely a rumor? Lafayette felt that he had gone too far to turn back now. With favorable winds blowing, he ordered *La Victoire* to set sail.

The busy harbor at Bordeaux, France, where Lafayette, Kalb, and the other French volunteers joined Lafayette's merchant ship, La Victoire.

They would leave French territorial waters, stop at a nearby Spanish port, and await further developments. *La Victoire* headed down the coast to San Sebastián, Spain. As the ship disappeared over the horizon, the government courier from Paris came galloping into Bordeaux.

At sea, Lafayette confessed to Kalb that he had never received his family's consent to go to America. The baron was surprised and upset. "If he had not been aboard the ship," Kalb wrote to his wife, "I think he would have gone home and, in my opinion, it would have been the right thing to do."

San Sebastián. To avoid the king's order forbidding his departure, Lafayette ordered La Victoire *to set sail for this Spanish port.*

In Bordeaux, when the king's courier learned that *La Victoire* had sailed, he reported to the port commandant, who had little trouble discovering the ship's destination. Again the courier was sent on his way, this time across the Spanish border. Three days later he arrived in San Sebastián, found *La Victoire* riding at anchor, and delivered the king's order to the unhappy young marquis.

By now Lafayette was having second thoughts. He had been ordered not to go to America by his family, by the king's ministers, and by the king himself. Even so, he had convinced himself that there must be a misunderstanding. If he could plead his case in person, perhaps he could persuade his father-in-law to change his mind. And if the duc d'Ayen withdrew his objections, the royal order might be rescinded. He told baron de Kalb that he wanted to return to Bordeaux, then go on to meet his father-in-law in Marseilles. There he would convince the duc that he must make the voyage to America.

"I have just had dinner with the marquis in San Sebastián," Kalb told his wife. "At this moment he has abandoned his trip to America and recanted his lust for war. He has left for Bordeaux. . . . I do not think he will return, and I advised him to sell the ship. . . . It is certain that this folly will cost him dearly. But if it be said that he has done a foolish thing, it may be answered that he acted from the most honorable motives and that he can hold up his head before all high-minded men."

Lafayette had boarded a coach bound for Bordeaux. During the bumpy three-day ride, he had plenty of time to mull over his predicament. By now, all France must have heard of his adventure. If he gave in, he would be a laughingstock.

Arriving in Bordeaux, he sent a letter to the French prime minister, pleading that the king's order be rescinded. Then he settled down to wait for an answer.

As word of Lafayette's return to France spread through Paris, the comte de Broglie, the man responsible for launching the young man's expedition, was not prepared to abandon the plan. If Lafayette didn't sail, then Kalb and the other French volunteers might never reach America. Lafayette's situation could undermine all those patient efforts to muster support for the American cause. Broglie dispatched a young officer, the vicomte de Mauroy, with orders to intercept Lafayette and encourage him to return to his ship.

Lafayette was still waiting for a reply from the prime minister when Mauroy reached Bordeaux. He told Lafayette that all Paris—except for his father-in-law—had acclaimed his great adventure. Everyone was watching to see what he would do. As for the king's order, it was issued only to appease Lafayette's family and reassure the British ambassador to France. Actually, Mauroy emphasized, neither the king nor anyone else was angry with Lafayette for "so noble an enterprise."

That was all the assurance Lafayette needed. He sent another letter to the prime minister, explaining that since he hadn't received a response to his earlier letter, he assumed that the minister's silence implied approval of his actions. Then he prepared to return to San Sebastián and the waiting *La Victoire.*

This time he would take no chances. Since the port commandant in Bordeaux had instructed Lafayette to report to military headquarters in Marseilles, Lafayette boarded the next coach to Marseilles. When the coachman stopped to change horses, he got out, disguised himself as a courier, bought a horse, and took off for Spain. During his ride back across the border, he was never sure whether the port commandant had sent French troops in pursuit. Along the way, he avoided public inns and slept beside his horse in out-of-the-way stables.

While waiting for Lafayette to return, Kalb had moved *La Victoire* to the more secluded harbor of Los Pasajes, close by San Sebastián. He was relieved when he saw the saddle-weary marquis gallop into the port. "Don't worry," Lafayette wrote to a friend as *La Victoire* was preparing to cast off, "once I have departed, everyone will agree with me; once I am victorious, everyone will applaud my enterprise."

Everyone was applauding long before he reached America. Lafayette's dramatic escape created a sensation in Paris. People spoke of little else. "It's undoubtedly an act of folly," said the marquise du Deffand, a prominent noblewoman, "but one which does him no dishonor and which, on the contrary, is characterized by courage and the desire for glory. People praise him more than they blame him."

Officially, the king's ministers were said to be outraged, but privately, they let it be known that they were not unduly disturbed by the actions of the wayward marquis. "I do not know whether the king is aware of [Lafayette's departure]," the French foreign minister told a friend. "I shall take good care not to speak to him about it."

Lafayette's departure "has occasioned much conversation here," Silas Deane reported to Congress, "and though the court pretends to know nothing of the matter, his conduct is highly extolled by the first people in France."

Even Marie Antoinette, who had once laughed at Lafayette, was now reported to admire his spirit.

La Victoire had lifted anchor and sailed from Los Pasajes for America on April 26, 1777, carrying Lafayette, fourteen other French officers, now including Mauroy, and a crew of thirty. The voyage across the Atlantic would take fifty-four tiresome days as the wind-tossed little vessel heaved and rolled through heavy seas, always on the lookout for privateers, pirates, and British warships. *La Victoire* had only two cannons, and was too heavy and slow to escape hostile ships or fight them off. To avoid capture by the British, who would be more severe with him than with an ordinary adventurer, Lafayette said he was prepared to "blow up" his ship rather than surrender.

But no threats materialized, and the voyage was uneventful. Lafayette spent the long days studying English and military tactics and adding daily installments to a long letter he was writing to Adrienne. "[H]aving to choose between the slavery that everyone believes he has the right to impose upon me, and liberty, which called me to glory, I departed," he wrote. "Have you forgiven me?" he asked more than once. "One day follows another here, and, what is worse, they are all alike. Always the sky, always the water, and again the next day the same thing."

Finally *La Victoire*'s crew sighted land, and the ship dropped anchor off a quiet South Carolina beach, a safe distance from the British warships that were blockading the entrance to Charleston Bay. When Lafayette stepped ashore on American soil for the first time on Friday, June 13, 1777, his troubles were not yet over. True enough, he had overcome the opposition of his own king and country. Now the nineteen-year-old major general would have to face the skepticism of the United States Congress.

Carrying Lafayette, fourteen other French volunteers, and a crew of thirty, La Victoire sails from Spain, heading for America. From a painting by Hubert Robert.

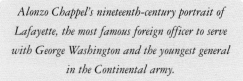

Alonzo Chappel's nineteenth-century portrait of Lafayette, the most famous foreign officer to serve with George Washington and the youngest general in the Continental army.

⚜ FIVE ⚜

"Here to Learn"

WITH *La Victoire* ANCHORED OFFSHORE, Lafayette, Kalb, and a few other officers climbed into the ship's launch and were rowed along the South Carolina coast. They were searching for a pilot who could bypass the British blockade and guide *La Victoire* to a safe harbor in Charleston, where the ship's cargo was to be unloaded and sold. They rowed for hours without finding any signs of life. At last they came upon a group of black slaves in a small boat who were dredging for oysters—the first people they had met since reaching the shores of America.

The slaves offered to take them to the house of their master, Benjamin Huger, a major in the South Carolina militia. It was almost midnight by the time they arrived. Huger emerged from his house holding a torch and flanked by barking guard dogs. After the French officers identified themselves, he invited them to spend the night.

"I retired to rest that night," Lafayette recalled, "rejoicing that I had at last attained the haven of my dreams and had landed in America beyond the reach of my pursuers."

The next morning, Huger found a pilot to steer *La Victoire* to Charleston. He advised Lafayette and his party to travel overland to avoid possible capture by the British at sea, and he furnished them with three horses. Taking turns riding and walking, the men set out for Charleston across seventy miles of trackless swamps and woods. Three days later "we arrived looking very much like beggars and brigands," a member of the party recalled. "People mocked us when we said we were French officers here to defend their liberty, and we were looked on as adventurers." But when Lafayette's ship sailed safely into port the following day, laden with goods from Europe, "their attitude turned full circle. The city's leading citizens opened their doors to us . . . for eight days of feasts and gala celebrations."

Lafayette sold his ship's cargo and arranged to send *La Victoire* back to France with a new cargo. Then he and his fellow officers set out for the American capital at Philadelphia in four newly purchased carriages, bouncing and lurching over rutted roads. "By the fourth day some of our carriages were in splinters," one of the men wrote in his diary. "Several of our horses, nearly all of which were old and weak, either died or went lame, and we had to buy others along the way. . . . We traveled a great part of the way on foot, often sleeping in the woods, starving, prostrated by the heat, and some of us suffered from fever and dysentery."

But nothing it seemed, no hardship, no discomfort, could dampen Lafayette's buoyant enthusiasm. "The farther north I go," he wrote to Adrienne, "the more I love this country and its people."

The French officers' 800-mile hike to Philadelphia—"no campaign in Europe could be more difficult than this journey," one of them complained—took thirty-two days. They reached the American capital on July 27 "in a much more pitiable condition than that in which we entered Charleston." The officers found lodging, brushed themselves off, and prepared to present their credentials to Congress.

The next morning they went to the Pennsylvania State House, where Congress was sitting, carrying Silas Deane's letters of recommendation along with contracts for the commissions he had promised. They waited at the statehouse door until Massachusetts Congressman James Lovell, chairman of the Committee on Foreign Applications, came outside to speak to them. Lovell did not waste time on pleasantries. He got right to

*The State House
in Philadelphia, where
Congress met in 1777.
Lafayette and his fellow
volunteers were turned
away at the door.*

the point. "It seems that French officers have a great fancy to enter our service without being invited," he said. "It is true that we were in need of officers last year, but now we have experienced men and plenty of them."

With that, Lovell turned on his heel and went back into the statehouse, leaving the speechless French officers standing in the street. "We did not know what to think," one of them wrote. "It is impossible to be more astounded than we were. . . . We decided to wait and seek the reason for this affront before we complained about it."

The earliest authenticated portrait of George Washington, painted by Charles Willson Peale in 1772, five years before Washington met Lafayette.

In the past year, Congress had been put off by the number of adventurers coming over from Europe, men of "unbounded pride and ambition," as Washington called them. Many fine European officers had volunteered for the American army; some were to give their lives for the rebels' cause. But other European volunteers turned out to be self-seeking soldiers of fortune who exaggerated their qualifications and demanded high ranks and inflated salaries. By the time Lafayette and his fellow officers showed up in Philadelphia, Congress was in no mood to accept further volunteers.

Lafayette and his companions knew nothing about the troubles the Americans had been having. But they knew very well that they had risked an ocean crossing and endured an arduous overland hike, only to be unceremoniously brushed off at the doors of Congress.

Congressman Lovell may have been reminded that Lafayette was no ordinary volunteer, because the next day he called on the French officers and apologized for the brusque reception they had received. And he promised that Congress would review their credentials carefully.

Lafayette appealed directly to Congress. "After the sacrifices I have made," he wrote, "I have the right to exact two favors: one is to serve at my own expense and the other is to begin to serve as a volunteer."

Congress agreed to grant Lafayette the major general's commission that Silas Deane had promised him. He would receive no pay or other compensation, as he himself had proposed. And because he lacked military experience, his rank was to be considered strictly honorary. He would not receive a responsible command unless Washington, as commander in chief, decided to give him one.

On July 31, 1777, Congress passed a resolution confirming the commission of the nineteen-year-old major general:

"Whereas the Marquis de Lafayette, out of his great zeal to the cause of liberty, in which the United States are engaged, has left his family and connections and at his own expense come over to offer his service to the United States without pension or particular allowance, and is anxious to risk his life in our cause: Resolved that his service be accepted and that in consideration of his zeal, illustrious family and connections, he have the rank and commission of major general in the army of the United States."

Lafayette's request to serve directly under General Washington was approved, and he was directed to report to Washington's headquarters just outside Philadelphia. At their first meeting, Lafayette was in awe of the towering American commander he had heard so much about. "Although [Washington] was surrounded by officers and citizens," Lafayette recalled, "it was impossible to mistake for a moment his majestic figure and deportment."

Invited to witness a review of the troops, Lafayette watched as "eleven thousand men poorly armed and even more poorly clothed" marched past. The soldiers wore every imaginable kind of clothing, from fringed hunting shirts and leather leggings to makeshift combinations of patched and tattered uniforms. "We should be embarrassed," said Washington, "to show ourselves to an officer who has just left the French army."

Lafayette snapped to attention. "I am here to learn, and not to teach," he told Washington.

Washington was pleased by this answer, but there was another reason for his embarrassment other than the threadbare condition of his army. He did not know what to do with this boy general who had never fired a shot in battle. Even so, he could not help liking the eager youth who appeared so anxious to join the American cause. Starting from that day, a friendship developed between the forty-five-year-old American commander who had never fathered a son, and the nineteen-year-old French nobleman who had never seen his father.

The war, meanwhile, was not going well for the American rebels. British troops were

A bootless American soldier in his patched and tattered uniform. Note his bare toes.

pushing down from Canada, attempting to take control of the Hudson River and sever the crucial supply line from New England to Washington's army and the revolutionary capital at Philadelphia. A second large British army was moving toward Philadelphia from the south. To reach the city the British would have to cross Brandywine Creek, where Washington would make his stand and Lafayette would have his first chance to prove his courage.

On September 11, 1777, Washington's troops were stretched out along the eastern bank of the Brandywine, ready to fight off the British army led by General William Howe. Because of confusing intelligence reports, Washington was caught by surprise when the British forded the Brandywine at two points, looped around, and attacked from the rear, threatening to encircle the Americans.

Five days after his twentieth birthday, Lafayette faced the test he had been preparing for all his life. Sensing that the main action would take place on the right flank of the American force, he saw a chance to distinguish himself. He asked Washington's permission to join General John Sullivan's men on the right; permission was granted, and he galloped off with his two aides.

"By the time [we] arrived, the enemy had crossed the ford," Lafayette recalled. "Sullivan's troops had barely enough time to form a line in front of a thin wood." As the British advanced, firing muskets and cannons, the Americans held their ground until the enemy troops were within twenty yards. Facing withering enemy fire, the American line wavered and then broke.

A British private, Elisha Stevens, recorded his impressions of the battle: "Cannons roaring muskets cracking drums beating bombs flying all round. Men a dying woundeds horred grones which would greave the heardist of hearts to see such a dollful sight as this to see our fellow creators slain in such a manner as this."

Lafayette had never before been under fire. Galloping back and forth, rearing his horse into the air, and finally jumping to the ground, he tried to halt the retreat. Men rallied around him and faced the enemy's charge but were overwhelmed by the sheer number of British troops. With dead and wounded men falling about them, the Americans were forced to fall back to the safety of the woods behind.

It was only then that Lafayette noticed blood seeping from his boot. In the noise and confusion of battle, he hadn't realized that a musket ball had torn through the calf of his left leg. He was helped back onto his horse, and as the Americans retreated he tried to rejoin Washington. But he was losing so much blood that he had to stop to have his wound bandaged. He barely escaped capture.

Falling darkness ended the fighting. Despite their bravery—the rebels had put up "a steady, stubborn fight from hill to hill and from wall to wall," said a British officer—Washington's troops had been forced into a general retreat to the town of Chester, twelve miles from the battlefield. During the retreat, Washington found Lafayette, weak from loss of blood, trying to organize some troops to defend a bridge over Chester Creek.

Lafayette lies wounded at the Battle of Brandywine Creek, September 11, 1777. From a nineteenth-century engraving by C. H. Jeens.

"The whole army this night retired to Chester," Colonel Timothy Pickering of Massachusetts wrote in his journal. "It was fortunate for us that the night came on, for under its cover the fatigued stragglers and some wounded made their escape." The Americans had suffered more than a thousand casualties, the British only half that many.

"Sir: I am sorry to inform you, that in this day's engagement, we have been obliged to leave the enemy masters of the field," Washington reported to the president of Congress. "Notwithstanding the misfortune of the day, I am happy to find the troops in good spirits, and I hope another time we shall compensate for the losses now sustained."

In Chester, Lafayette had his wound dressed and rebandaged by Washington's personal physician. The following day, as he was being loaded onto a boat to be transported up the Delaware River to Philadelphia, where his wound could be properly treated, he heard Washington tell the physician, "Treat him as if he were my son."

❧ Six ❧

Winter at Valley Forge

AFTER THE AMERICAN DEFEAT at Brandywine, Washington warned Congress that he could not defend Philadelphia. The worried lawmakers packed up and fled the city, taking up temporary quarters in the country town of York, Pennsylvania, more than a hundred miles away. Lafayette was sent by boat and carriage from Philadelphia to a hospital in Bethlehem, Pennsylvania, where he would be out of harm's way while he recovered from his wound. On September 26, 1777—two weeks after the Battle of Brandywine—British troops marched into Philadelphia and occupied America's biggest city and revolutionary capital.

As Lafayette lay bedridden in Bethlehem, his wounded leg still painful and oozing, he learned that Washington had suffered another defeat. On October 4, the rebel army had attempted to surprise the British at Germantown, just outside Philadelphia. Confused by a dense fog and by the smoke and chaos of battle, the Americans fired on one another and were forced to retreat, losing another thousand men who were killed or taken prisoner.

The Battle of Germantown, October 4, 1777: another American defeat. From an 1853 illustration in Harper's Weekly.

General Nathanael Greene offered Lafayette
his first independent battlefield command. From
a painting by Charles Willson Peale.

Lafayette was impatient to return to action. And now that he had been wounded in battle, he felt he was ready to take on the command of an army division. "Consider, if you please, that Europe and particularly France is looking upon me," he wrote to Washington in his still imperfect English. "That I want to do some thing by myself, and justify that love of glory which I let be known to the world in making those sacrifices which have appeared so surprising, some say foolish. Do not you think that this want is right?. . . I would deserve the reproachs [sic] of my friends and family if I would . . . stay in a country where I could not find the occasions of distinguishing myself."

Still limping, his leg too painful for him to pull on his boot, he climbed out of his sickbed, bought a horse, and galloped off to join Washington's encampment outside Philadelphia. By the time he arrived, British troops had scored yet another victory, capturing the American forts along the Delaware River. British ships could now sail freely upriver to Philadelphia and beyond.

In November, Washington ordered General Nathanael Greene to set out on a reconnaissance mission and determine the strength of British outposts around Philadelphia. Lafayette, his leg healed, volunteered to join the mission. Greene, who had seen for himself Lafayette's courage at Brandywine, had become fond of the young Frenchman. "He is one of the sweetest-tempered young gentleman," Greene wrote to his wife, "he has left a young wife and a fine fortune . . . to come and engage in the cause of liberty—this is a noble enthusiasm."

Leading four hundred riflemen—his first independent battlefield command—Lafayette crept through the woods with his men, came upon a British outpost, and boldly attacked, driving the enemy troops back to their base. In his report to Washington, General Greene praised Lafayette's handling of the engagement—his courage, coolness, and skill against more experienced British officers and a larger force. "The Marquis is determined to be in the way of danger," Greene wrote.

The skirmish was a small victory, but it convinced Washington that Lafayette had the ability to take on a command appropriate to his rank of major general. He urged Congress to grant the marquis command of a division. "He is more and more solicitous to be in actual service," Washington wrote, "and is pressing his application for a command. . . . I feel a refusal would not only induce him to return {to France} in disgust, but may involve some unfavorable consequences." If Lafayette were to go back to France disappointed, Washington feared, French support for the American cause might suffer. Congress agreed. On December 1, 1777, it was resolved that "It is highly agreeable to Congress that the Marquis de la Fayette be appointed to the command of a division in the Continental army."

At twenty, his rank no longer simply "honorary," Lafayette was the Continental army's youngest general. Washington offered him command of any division he chose. He picked a division of Virginians, from the commander in chief's home state.

As the season's first snow fell on the Pennsylvania countryside, Washington prepared to move his bedraggled troops to a wooded plateau called the Valley Forge, where the Continental army would settle into its winter quarters. Washington had chosen the site because it afforded plenty of timber with which to build wooden huts to shelter his men during the harsh Pennsylvania winter. The elevated plateau could be readily defended. It was close enough to Philadelphia to allow the rebels to keep a close watch on the British and harass them at every opportunity. Most important, the isolated winter camp would give Washington a chance to rebuild his army and rest his weary soldiers, who were short of food, clothing, blankets, and just about everything else.

The men went to work felling trees and sawing timber. Within a few weeks more than two thousand log huts had been built standing side by side in orderly rows, each with a fireplace at one end and a doorway at the other facing a brigade "street." "By skillfully arranging the trunks of small trees, they built a town of wood there . . . and the whole army settled into its melancholy winter quarters," Lafayette recalled. Each

Lafayette and Washington at Valley Forge during the winter of 1777-1778. From an 1857 illustration by Alonzo Chappel.

hut accommodated twelve enlisted men, who slept on straw mattresses in double-decker bunks. Officers' huts had fewer occupants, depending on rank. As a major general, Lafayette had a hut to himself. Washington moved into a small stone farmhouse, which became his command headquarters.

The log huts afforded protection from the biting winter winds that whipped across the frozen plateau, but with the shortage of provisions, the basic challenge for every ragged, ill-fed fighting man was how to survive the winter. "The unfortunate American soldiers lacked everything," Lafayette recalled, "—coats, hats, shirts, and shoes. Their feet and legs turned black with frostbite and often had to be amputated. . . . The army lacked provisions for entire days, and the patient endurance of the officers and men was a continuous miracle, constantly renewed."

Lafayette shared the hardships with the men of his division. He ate the same unsalted boiled beef, when it was available, and spent his own money to buy them shoes and warm clothing. He was now the junior member of what Washington called his "military family," along with twenty-two-year-old Alexander Hamilton and twenty-three-year-old John Laurens, whose father, Henry, was president of the Continental Congress. Hamilton and Laurens were both fluent in French, Lafayette's English was improving, and the three young officers became the best of friends and Washington's closest aides.

Lafayette came to admire Washington greatly. "The better I know him the more I venerate him," he wrote to his wife. And in a letter to his father-in-law, the duc d'Ayens, Lafayette said, "Our general is a man truly made for this revolution, which could not succeed without him." He urged his father-in-law to use his influence at the French court to gain more aid for the Americans. "We are not, I confess, as strong as I expected," he wrote, "but we are able to fight and we shall do so, I hope, with some success. With the help of France, we shall win, at some expense, the cause that I cherish because it is just, because it honors humanity, because it is in the interest of my nation, and because my American friends and I are deeply committed to it."

In January 1778, Lafayette learned that Congress was planning an expedition to drive the British out of Canada and bring that vast northern territory into the American union. A former French colony called New France, and still largely French-speaking, Canada had been lost to the British some fifteen years earlier, during the Seven Years' War. Lafayette had dreamed of leading an invasion of Canada to expel the British, and Congress decided to put him in charge of the campaign. The recapture of

John Laurens and Alexander Hamilton. Along with Lafayette, they were members of Washington's close-knit "military family."

A letter Lafayette wrote to George Washington on December 31, 1777, soon after the Continental army had pitched camp at Valley Forge.

New France by an American force led by a French nobleman would encourage French support for the rebels' cause. "The idea of liberating all of New France . . . is too glorious for me to allow myself to dwell upon it," he wrote to his wife.

Through no fault of Lafayette's, the hastily planned invasion of Canada was doomed from the beginning and would have been a disaster if carried out. Lafayette traveled through ice and snow from Valley Forge to Albany, New York, the expedition's staging point. When he reached Albany on February 17, he found neither the troops nor the supplies he had been promised. Fewer than half of the 2,500 men he was expecting had reported for duty. There wasn't nearly enough clothing, provisions, ammunition, sledges, or snowshoes, and the season was already too advanced to wait for the needed supplies.

Lafayette had been warned not to embark on this expedition, but his dreams of glory had clouded his judgment. Now he was advised against going on. "I have consulted everybody," he wrote to Washington, "and everybody answers me that I should be mad to undertake this operation." It seemed that everyone in America and in France knew that he had been appointed to lead the invasion of Canada; in calling it off, he felt humiliated. "My situation is such that I am reduced to wish to have never put the foot in America," he complained to Henry Laurens, president of Congress. "Men will have the right to laugh at me, and I'll be almost ashamed to appear before some. . . . No, sir, this expedition will certainly reflect a little upon my reputation . . . but it will reflect much more upon the authors of such blunders."

He appealed to Washington for support: "Why am I so far from you," he wrote, "and what business had [Congress] to hurry me through the ice and snow without knowing what I should do, neither what they were doing themselves?"

Washington tried to reassure him: "It will be no disadvantage to you to have it known in Europe, that you had received so manifest a proof of the good opinion and confidence of Congress as an important detached command—and I am persuaded that everyone will applaud your prudence [in calling off the invasion]."

An Iroquois council fire as depicted in a 1901 issue of Harper's Weekly.

Lafayette's trip to the north was not a total loss, however. While he was in Albany, waiting for men and supplies that never arrived, he had a chance to attend a gathering of the Six Nations (also known as the Iroquois Confederacy), the Indian tribes of New York: Mohawks, Oneidas, Senecas, Cayugas, Tuscaroras, and Onondagas. Congress had appointed General Philip Schuyler to meet with the tribes and gain their support in the war against the British. The Iroquois had once been allies of France who fought British expansion into their territory, and Iroquois leaders still regarded the French with respect.

Schuyler invited Lafayette to accompany him, and they traveled by sleigh to Johnson's Town (now Johnstown), New York, where some of the tribes had gathered by the Mohawk River. "Five hundred men, women and children attended the convention," Lafayette recalled, "streaked with multi-colored paint and feathers. . . . The old men smoked and talked about politics intelligently. . . . Their goal was a balance of power."

Lafayette and Schuyler spent several days conferring with Indian elders, smoking their peace pipes, exchanging gifts, and finally concluding a treaty of friendship. Lafayette's manner and his generosity so impressed the Oneidas that they adopted him into their tribe and named him Kayewla, after one of their greatest warriors.

When Lafayette returned to Valley Forge after an absence of two months, he found that conditions at the camp had changed dramatically for the better. To the surprise of nearly everyone, the threadbare Continental army had held together through the worst hardships of the winter. Washington, meeting with delegations of congressmen who came to inspect the winter encampment, had demanded a complete overhaul of the army's supply system. At his insistence, the quartermaster and commissary departments, which were responsible for feeding and clothing the troops, had been reorganized under new leadership. As a result, the camp was now overflowing with supplies. Fresh uniforms were arriving, and the men were at last beginning to eat well.

The troops, meanwhile, had been whipped into military shape by another foreign volunteer, a veteran of the Prussian army by the name of Friedrich Wilhelm August Heinrich Ferdinand, baron von Steuben. Though he spoke almost no English, Steuben possessed a deep knowledge of European military procedures and a passion for drilling troops on the parade ground. He knew how to train an army. During week after week of rigorous drilling, he transformed the farmers and backwoodsmen of Washington's army into a disciplined European-style fighting force with the confidence to compete on equal terms with professional British troops.

Throughout the winter, Lafayette had been sending a steady stream of letters to France, urging everyone he knew to support the American cause. By now he was seen as a hero—the wealthy young nobleman who had forsaken fortune, friends, and family to cross the Atlantic and fight for liberty. Even his father-in-law, the duc d'Ayen, had been won over and boasted about Gilbert's accomplishments. "The very persons who blamed him most for his bold enterprise now applauded him," wrote Lafayette's friend the comte de Ségur. "The court showed itself almost proud of him, and all the young men envied him."

In Paris, meanwhile, Benjamin Franklin had joined Silas Deane and Arthur Lee as one of the American commissioners seeking an alliance with France. On May 1, 1778, Deane's brother, Simeon, galloped into Washington's Valley Forge headquarters bearing sensational news. France had recognized the independence of the United States! Treaties of friendship and alliance between the two countries had been signed in Paris on February 6. News of the treaties, carried by sailing ship across the Atlantic, had taken nearly three months to reach Valley Forge.

German-born General Friedrich von Steuben: His rigorous drills at Valley Forge, depicted in the painting by Edwin Austin Abbey, transformed the American army into a disciplined and confident fighting force.

Winter at Valley Forge

Lafayette was so excited when he heard the news that he lost all command of his hard-won English. Writing to Henry Laurens, he exclaimed, "Very happy I find myself to see things so well brought to the common and glory and satisfaction."

"Very happy" he might have been, but the war was not yet over, and the alliance with France did not guarantee an American victory.

❧ Seven ❧

The Battles of Barren Hill and Monmouth Courthouse

ALL WINTER, Washington had been expecting an attack on Valley Forge by the British forces occupying Philadelphia, just twenty miles away, but a British offensive never materialized. General Howe, the cautious British commander, kept his army at a distance from the strongly fortified American camp.

Washington's spies reported that Howe, having failed to destroy the American army, was about to be replaced as commander in chief by General Henry Clinton. Rumor had it that Clinton was expecting thousands of reinforcements. To find out what the British were up to, Washington put Lafayette in charge of a reconnaissance force that would spy on them. He was to move as close as possible to Philadelphia and report any sudden or unexpected movement by the enemy. The assignment was Washington's way of showing confidence in the twenty-year-old major general after the failure of his Canadian expedition.

Lafayette left Valley Forge on the morning of May 18, 1778, with 2,200 specially chosen troops and five cannons—the largest force he had ever commanded. Among the troops were forty-seven Oneida Indian scouts, "stout-looking fellows and remarkably neat," according to Private Joseph Plumb Martin, a member of

British general Sir William Howe (left), having failed to destroy Washington's army, was replaced in Philadelphia by General Henry Clinton.

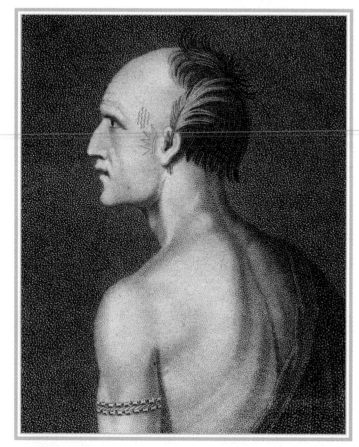

An 1801 French engraving of an Oneida warrior. Lafayette's Oneida scouts held off a British cavalry charge.

the expedition. The Oneidas had met Lafayette in northern New York at the gathering of the Iroquois Confederacy earlier that year and had volunteered to serve under General Washington at Valley Forge.

Lafayette established a base camp at Barren Hill, a steep-sided ridge that, he believed, could be readily defended. He sent out patrols to range through the nearby woods and seize anyone who might be spying on the camp. He was now about two miles from the nearest British outpost and within twelve miles of Philadelphia.

All was quiet until the morning of May 20. A low fog shrouded the woods and meadows around Barren Hill. At dawn the sound of hoof-beats, then gunfire, alerted everyone that a surprise British attack was under way. "We were told that the British were advancing upon us in our rear," Private Martin recalled. "How they could get there was to us a mystery, but they *were* there."

The day before, a deserter from Lafayette's force had made his way to Philadelphia and informed the British where the Americans were camped and who was in command. General Howe had not yet turned over his command to General Clinton. Howe now saw his chance to silence his critics and cap his career by bringing home the young noble-man who had come to symbolize the alliance between France and America.

Howe postponed his departure from Philadelphia. He mustered eight thousand men—three-fourths of his army—and marched to Barren Hill at night, accompanied by General Clinton, who went along as a spectator. He planned to ambush Lafayette, capture him, take him to Philadelphia, then carry him back to England as a prize. Howe was so confident of success that he "had invited the ladies [of Philadelphia] to dine with Lafayette the following night."

As the British strike force approached Barren Hill through the fog, Lafayette realized

Lafayette leads his troops in this idealized 1901 portrait by Edward Percy Moran. Note the dead British soldier lying by Lafayette's feet.

that his only chance was to lead his men on a rapid retreat toward the Schuylkill River. "The enemy had nearly surrounded us by the time our retreat commenced," Private Martin wrote, "but the road we were on was very favorable for us, being for the most part . . . through small woods and copses. . . . We crossed the Schuylkill in good order."

British cavalrymen brandishing sabers galloped after the retreating Americans. They were held off by the Oneida scouts, who let loose with hair-raising war whoops, startling both enemy horsemen and their steeds. The horses bolted, giving the Americans time to reach the river safely.

At Valley Forge, lookouts atop watchtowers had spotted the retreat and sounded the alarm. Within minutes, thanks in part to Steuben's systematic drilling, the entire American army was ready to march to Lafayette's aid. Seeing that they were now outnumbered, the British called off their attack.

Lafayette had learned nothing about the enemy's intentions—the purpose of his expedition—but he had managed to get away with his men without being captured or killed. And he had demonstrated great skill at deceiving the enemy, having his snipers change position after each shot to create the impression of a much larger force as his men made their way to safety. Washington praised his tactics. The marquis had been caught in a "snare . . . but because of his own dexterity, or the enemy's want of it, he disengaged himself in a very soldier-like manner," Washington reported.

Even so, it was a narrow escape. To prove that he hadn't been intimidated, Lafayette insisted on returning to Barren Hill the next day and spending the night there, as though he were thumbing his nose at General Howe.

Soon afterward, Washington heard rumors that the British were preparing to leave Philadelphia. He realized the rumors were true when one of his spies told him that British officers in Philadelphia had instructed their washerwomen to return their laundry at once, "finished or unfinished." A British evacuation was about to begin.

General Clinton, the new British commander, had learned that a French fleet was on its way to aid the Americans. When it arrived, French warships could blockade Philadelphia's harbor and trap the British army occupying the city. Clinton decided to pull out before the French could arrive, and to concentrate his forces in New York.

British ships loaded with troops and equipment sailed from Philadelphia on the morning of June 18. The rest of the occupying army, some nine thousand troops led by Clinton, prepared to march overland across New Jersey to New York, trailing a thousand supply wagons that stretched out behind them for twelve miles.

As General Clinton and his army marched out of Philadelphia, Washington put Lafayette in command of a four-thousand-man advance force with orders to snipe at Clinton's rear columns "or otherwise annoy the enemy." This was the largest army Lafayette had commanded so far. "The young Frenchman . . . moves toward the enemy . . . in rapture with his command and burning to distinguish himself," one of his aides reported.

On the morning of June 28, Washington's main army caught up with the British near the village of Monmouth Courthouse (now Freehold, New Jersey). Washington ordered an all-out attack, and the armies clashed amid smoke and confusion in sweltering hundred-degree heat. Early in the battle, the American general Charles Lee ordered a retreat. An enraged Washington galloped across the field and, as British artillery shells tore up the

Washington rallies his troops at the Battle of Monmouth Courthouse. From an 1852 painting by Emanuel Gottleib Leutze.

earth around him, dismissed Lee, took command of the battle, and rallied his troops to make a stand. He rode "all along the lines amid the shouts of the soldiers, cheering them by his voice and example and restoring to our standard the fortune of the fight," Lafayette reported. "I thought . . . that never had I beheld so superb a man."

The armies fought all day in smoke and dust under a searing sun, attacking and counter-attacking, as scores of soldiers on both sides were killed or wounded or died of heatstroke. At one point Lafayette's company was almost surrounded, but he was able to keep his men together as they moved toward a more secure position and avoided capture.

At dusk, fading light ended the fighting, and Washington ordered his men to get some rest. That night he slept among his troops. Spreading his cloak under an apple tree, he chatted quietly with Lafayette about the day's events until both men fell asleep.

By morning, the British had vanished. During the night, they had slipped away under cover of darkness. Washington decided it was unwise to push his exhausted troops and chase the enemy all the way to New York. The Americans claimed victory at Monmouth. They had fought the British to a standstill and forced them into a headlong retreat across New Jersey. And they had proved that they now had the training and dis-cipline to hold their own against seasoned British regulars in open battle.

In terms of manpower—each side fielded about thirteen thousand troops—Monmouth was the biggest one-day battle of the war. It was also the last major battle to take place in the north. In the months to come, fighting shifted to the southern colonies, where Lafayette would play a key role in the decisive battle of the Revolutionary War.

✤ EIGHT ✤

Hero of Two Worlds

ELEVEN DAYS AFTER the Battle of Monmouth, a French fleet with sixteen warships carrying four thousand troops sailed into Chesapeake Bay, but it didn't do much to help the American cause. The fleet's original mission had been to blockade Philadelphia's harbor. Since the British had already left the city, Washington proposed an alternative plan—a joint French-American attack on the isolated British garrison at Newport, Rhode Island.

The French ships headed north, where they encountered a violent storm. One ship sank. Others lost a mast, a rudder, or both, and had to be towed to Boston for repairs. By the time the ships were fit for service again, the fleet had been ordered to sail to the West Indies for the winter, and Washington had abandoned his plan to attack the British base at Newport.

Lafayette was deeply disappointed by the failure of the Newport expedition. He had expected to command an American detachment that would have fought alongside French infantrymen. Now, with no new battles in sight, his ambitions turned again to Canada. Although his first attempt to lead an invasion of Canada had been a humiliating failure, he was convinced that with enough troops and equipment, a joint French-American invasion could succeed. If he returned to France, he could convince the French government to support such a plan.

*Eighteenth-century
French warships.*

*As an American
envoy in Paris,
Benjamin Franklin
worked with
Lafayette to gain
French military and
financial support.*

Washington was doubtful, but some members of Congress seemed receptive. Lafayette exerted all his personal charm and powers of persuasion to win congressional approval. After weeks of hearings, Congress instructed Benjamin Franklin in Paris to work with Lafayette in gaining French support for a joint invasion of Canada.

Lafayette was granted a leave of absence from the Continental army. A ship, appropriately named the *Alliance*, was placed at his disposal for his voyage home. Congress sent him off with a resolution praising his service to America and a letter to King Louis XVI saying, "We recommend this young nobleman to your majesty's notice as one whom we know to be wise in counsel, gallant in the field, and patient under the hardships of war."

Lafayette returned to France on February 6, 1779, after an absence of two years. Since he had left the country in defiance of the king's orders, a royal punishment was necessary, and he was placed under house arrest in Paris for eight days. The house in question was the expansive Noailles mansion belonging to his wife's family, where the returning hero spent a triumphant confinement receiving visits from relatives and friends. Some friends hardly recognized him. He had left France as a boyish teenager; he returned prematurely balding and visibly aged by the rigors of the American winter and the stress of battle.

Adrienne, now nineteen, welcomed her husband tearfully. "My joy is impossible to describe," she wrote to Lafayette's aunts in Chavaniac. "[He] has come back to me as modest and as charming as when he went away. . . . God has preserved, in the midst of tremendous dangers, the most lovable person in the world."

The Noailles family mansion in Paris, where Lafayette was confined to "house arrest."

Lafayette wrote a letter of apology to King Louis XVI: "Love of my country, the desire to witness the humiliation of her enemies, and political feelings that the last treaty {with America} would seem to justify; these, Sire, are the reasons that governed the part I took in the American cause." When his house arrested ended, Louis summoned Lafayette to Versailles for an audience. The king delivered a mild reprimand, then forgave Lafayette, congratulated him on his success in America, and invited him to join a royal hunting party.

Welcomed at court, the twenty-one-year-old marquis was now consulted by the king's ministers, who recognized him as an authority on the situation in America and as a close personal friend of the legendary George Washington.

"I had left as a rebel and fugitive and returned in triumph as an idol," Lafayette recalled in his memoirs. Standing tall and proud in the handsome blue, white, and gold uniform of an American major general, chatting easily about America, its people, and the progress of the war, discussing his battle experiences against France's foremost enemy, England, Lafayette became the toast of Paris. Street minstrels sang ballads about his exploits. His appearance at the theater or opera was greeted with standing ovations. The once-laughable dancing partner of Marie Antoinette was now hailed as "the hero of two worlds."

Lafayette enjoyed the public acclaim, but he did not lose sight of his mission to rally French support for the American revolution, "whose success," he noted, "was still very much in doubt." Soon after his return to France, he learned that his hoped-for Canadian expedition had in the end been rejected by Congress. Washington had opposed the invasion as "not only too expensive and beyond our abilities, but too complex."

Putting the Canadian expedition aside, Lafayette turned to the prospect of sending a huge French expeditionary force across the Atlantic to aid the Americans—an expedition that he himself hoped to command. "Don't forget," he told the French foreign minister, the comte de Vergennes, "that I love the trade of war passionately, that I consider myself born especially to play that game, that I have been spoiled for two years by the habit of having been in command and of winning great confidence."

At home, meanwhile, amid the lavish comforts of the Noialles mansion, Lafayette had time to become reacquainted with the young wife he had left behind—and to embrace for the first time their daughter Anastasie, born when he was in America. Their first daughter, Henriette, had died at the age of two while he was at Valley Forge. On Christmas Eve 1779, Adrienne gave birth to their third child, a son. They named the boy George Washington and asked the infant's namesake to be his godfather. In a hasty note to Benjamin Franklin scribbled at two o'clock in the morning after the baby's birth, Lafayette was so flustered and excited he lost command of his English: "I don't loose time in informing You that Mde. de Lafayette is happily delivered of a son, and too much depend on your friendship not to be certain that you will be pleased with the intelligence. The boy will be call'd George, and you will easely gess that he bears that Name as a tribute of Respect and love for my dear friend Genl. Washington."

Lafayette and Washington wrote to each other often and at length. Despite the formalities of eighteenth-century correspondence, it is clear from the deeply personal tone of their letters that the two men missed each other. "I ardently wish I might be there next by you," Lafayette wrote. "I beg you would present my best compliments to your family, and remind them of my tender affection for them all. . . . Farewell, my dear general, and let our mutual affection last forever."

In one of the longest personal letters he ever wrote, Washington assured Lafayette that he "kept you constantly in remembrance," and that his feelings of affection "had ripened into perfect love & gratitude that neither time nor absence can impair."

For more than a year, meanwhile, Lafayette persisted in his efforts to gain French aid for the American rebels. He repeatedly urged the king's minister to send a massive naval and military force to America. His lengthy letters to Vergennes, the foreign minister, and the comte de Maurepas, the prime minister, his numerous personal visits to the

Lafayette's son, George Washington Lafayette. Detail from an eighteenth-century French painting.

palace at Versailles, and his meetings with Benjamin Franklin in Paris, finally brought results. The king's ministers agreed to organize an expedition and opened talks with Franklin for new loans to the United States.

Lafayette, however, was deemed too young and inexperienced to lead such an important mission. The command was assigned to Jean-Baptiste-Donatien de Vimeur, the comte de Rochambeau, who had held the rank of major general in the French army almost since Lafayette was born. Lafayette was to serve as liaison between Rochambeau and Washington.

Lafayette boarded a French frigate bound for America on March 5, 1780, well ahead of the French expeditionary force, which was still being organized. He was instructed to resume his command in the American army and inform Washington that a large French fleet with thousands of troops would soon be on its way.

Charles Willson Peale's realistic portrait of Lafayette as he appeared in 1779, prematurely balding at the age of twenty-two.

❧ NINE ❧

"The Boy Cannot Escape Me"

LANDING AT MARBLEHEAD, MASSACHUSETTS, on April 27, 1780, Lafayette jumped ashore and scribbled a hasty note to Washington: "Here I am, my dear general, and in the midst of the joy I feel in finding myself again one of your loving soldiers . . . I have affairs of the utmost importance which I should at first communicate to you alone. . . . Adieu, my dear general; you will easily know the hand of your young soldier."

When Lafayette reached Washington's headquarters at Morristown, New Jersey, two weeks later, he learned that the Continental army had endured another punishing winter, the coldest in memory, and was again short of food and clothing. In the north, the war had reached a stalemate, marked by small, inconclusive engagements that fizzled out and settled nothing. British troops had evacuated their isolated base at Newport, moving their cannons, equipment, and supplies south to General Clinton's heavily fortified headquarters in New York City. The main scene of action had shifted to the south, where a British offensive had overrun Georgia and South Carolina and was threatening North Carolina and Virginia.

Washington welcomed the news that the French navy was on its way with troops and supplies. Without massive French aid, there was little hope of winning the war. But when the French fleet under Rochambeau finally sailed into Newport harbor in

French troops commanded by the comte de Rochambeau disembark at Newport, Rhode Island. From a 1784 German etching.

July, two months after Lafayette told Washington it was coming, it was carrying far fewer troops and supplies than Washington had expected. To avoid a British blockade of French ports, Rochambeau had left behind two regiments and the ships to transport them. Washington had hoped to collaborate with the French in an attack on British-occupied New York, but he now agreed with Rochambeau that their combined forces were too small to risk such an attack. A major offensive would have to wait until the French could establish clear naval superiority, break the British blockade, and send additional ships and troops as reinforcements.

Lafayette, meanwhile, was placed in command of an elite corps of two thousand picked troops. He bought distinctive new uniforms for the men, trained them in daily drills to flawless parade-ground standards, and inspired in them an esprit de corps that became known as the best in the army. "The confidence and attachment of the troops are to him priceless possessions, hard-won riches," a French visitor observed. But while Lafayette was justifiably proud of his Light Division, he continued to be frustrated in his yearning for action. Impatiently, he wanted to organize a surprise attack on British troops at the northern tip of New York Island (now Manhattan). Washington vetoed the plan as too risky. And he rejected any further attacks in the north until French reinforcements could arrive.

Early in 1781, Lafayette had his chance to see some action. Washington sent him south with 1,200 of his men to help defend Virginia. British troops led by the American traitor Benedict Arnold were rampaging across the state, plundering and burning warehouses, foundries, and mills. Lafayette was ordered to capture Arnold, if he could, and hang him for treason. He reached Virginia in time to fight off a British assault on the city of Richmond. Spreading his troops widely across an embankment in front of the city, and having them jump from one position to another between shots as they kept up a rapid rain of fire, he fooled the British into thinking that he had twice as many men as he actually had.

But he soon faced a much stronger enemy. Lord Charles Cornwallis, commanding England's main southern army, marched his troops up from North Carolina to take charge of the campaign in Virginia. Cornwallis replaced Benedict Arnold, who returned to British-occupied New York, escaping capture and saving his neck.

Cornwallis was supremely confident that he could crush Lafayette's small force of Continentals and Virginia militiamen. He vowed to capture the young Frenchman and carry him back to England in chains. "The boy cannot escape me," he boasted. "I shall now proceed to dislodge [him] from Richmond."

Lafayette was outnumbered by about four to one. He was expecting reinforcements, but at the moment he could not risk a full-scale battle. The possibility "of a general defeat . . . has rendered me extremely cautious in my movements," he reported to Washington. "I am not strong enough even to get beaten."

Facing overwhelming odds, Lafayette pulled his troops out of Richmond and retreated into the Virginia countryside. The best he could hope for until reinforcements reached him was to keep his casualties as low as possible. As Cornwallis pursued him,

Colonel Benedict Arnold. An American traitor, he led British troops who fought against Lafayette in Virginia. From a 1776 portrait by Thomas Hart.

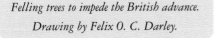

*Felling trees to impede the British advance.
Drawing by Felix O. C. Darley.*

Lafayette relied on a cat-and-mouse strategy of evasion, moving his men through thick brush and along heavily wooded slopes, felling trees and destroying bridges behind them to impede the enemy's advance. Snipers hiding behind bushes and in trees fired on advancing British columns, then vanished into the forest. "Were I to fight a battle, I would be cut to pieces," Lafayette reported. "Were I to decline fighting, the country would think itself given up. I am therefore determined to skirmish, but not to engage too far." Cornwallis failed to trap Lafayette, and nearly exhausted his troops trying to catch the elusive Frenchman.

In June, the British commander received new orders: he was to march his army to the Virginia coast and build a deepwater port on Chesapeake Bay, to be used as a naval base for a future attack on Philadelphia. As Cornwallis and his army slogged across inland Virginia, heading for the sea, Lafayette and his troops followed at a distance, harassing the British rear guard, striking with swift hit-and-run attacks, always giving

*General Charles Cornwallis expected to capture Lafayette but found himself
cornered at Yorktown. From a portrait by John Singleton Copley.*

the impression that the American force was larger than it was. Lafayette wasn't strong enough to risk a pitched battle, but as Cornwallis advanced toward the coast with the Americans trailing him cautiously, word spread all along the route that Lafayette was driving the enemy before him.

The impression that the Americans were chasing the British encouraged local militiamen to join Lafayette's force. He picked up strength every day. Then his promised reinforcements arrived, and by the beginning of July his little army had swelled to almost 2,500 well-equipped infantrymen, cavalrymen, and artillerymen. And he had fooled people (including some future historians) into thinking that he had driven Cornwallis out of most of Virginia.

Cornwallis picked the village of Yorktown as the site for the deepwater port. While his troops built defensive fortifications, Lafayette set up a ring of artillery positions around Yorktown to prevent a British breakout by land. "Should a French fleet now come [to Chesapeake Bay] . . . the British army would, I think, be ours," he reported to Washington. Cornwallis didn't realize it yet, but he had painted himself into a corner; he would not escape "the boy."

Up north, Washington received word that the long-awaited French reinforcements were on their way. A flotilla of twenty-nine warships carrying three thousand troops had sailed from the French West Indies under the command of Admiral François-Joseph-Paul, the comte de Grasse. Washington had been planning to mount a major offensive against the British in New York, but instead of heading for New York the French ships were sailing toward Chesapeake Bay, where Lafayette had cornered Cornwallis at the tip of the Yorktown peninsula.

Even with reinforcements, General Rochambeau in Newport had argued, a combined French-American army would not be strong enough to overcome the British fortifications guarding New York. Yorktown seemed a more tempting target. If Grasse's warships could blockade the entrance to Chesapeake Bay near the mouth of the York

River, Cornwallis would be trapped on the peninsula, between the French-American land force facing him and the York River at his back.

Washington agreed to scrap his plan for an attack against New York and to join forces with Rochambeau and march south to Virginia. He wrote to Lafayette, informing him that a French fleet was on its way and that a combined French-American land force would soon be on the march. He ordered Lafayette to stand firm, to "do all in your power to prevent [Cornwallis's] escape by land."

Marching south from Newport, Rochambeau's troops joined Washington's army in New Jersey, and the combined allied land force headed to Virginia. French heavy artillery, needed to bombard British defenses at Yorktown, was being shipped from Newport by sea. Grasse's warships, meanwhile, had reached Chesapeake Bay and in a ferocious daylong sea battle had driven off a British fleet that had sailed down from New York. The French navy now was in full command of the Chesapeake and its surrounding waters, and French troops had gone ashore to reinforce Lafayette.

Grasse urged Lafayette not to wait for Washington to arrive, but to storm Yorktown at once. Cornwallis could not escape, he argued. An immediate victory would give Lafayette the lion's share of the glory for what promised to be the decisive battle of the war. But out of loyalty to Washington and concern for his troops, Lafayette insisted on waiting, his passion for glory tempered now by the responsibilities of leadership. "The temptation was great," he

French and British warships clash near the mouth of Chesapeake Bay, September 5, 1781. By driving off the British fleet, the French gained control of the sea off Yorktown. This drawing by J. O. Davidson appeared in the commemorative issue of Harper's Weekly, September 5, 1881.

admitted later, "but even if the attack had succeeded, it would necessarily have cost a good deal of blood."

By the time Washington and Rochambeau reached the Yorktown peninsula in mid-September, the allied force, bolstered by Virginia and Maryland militia, totaled nearly twenty thousand men. Preparations for the siege of Yorktown continued for some three weeks as the French and Americans dug trenches, built fortifications, and dragged their heavy siege guns into position. The allied army arranged itself before Yorktown with the French on the left, the Americans on the right. Lafayette commanded one of the three American divisions. Serving under him as regimental commanders were his two close friends Colonels Alexander Hamilton and John Laurens.

Beginning on October 9, the siege guns pounded the British fortifications day and night as allied troops crept closer to the enemy's front lines. Two British outposts— redoubts nine and ten—blocked their path. On October 14, Washington ordered that the two outposts be stormed by bayonet; he assigned redoubt number nine to the French and number ten to Lafayette's infantrymen. The officer in charge of the French assault grandly informed Lafayette that he would be happy to send him reinforcements if he needed them. But the American assault, led by Hamilton, captured redoubt ten so quickly that Lafayette enjoyed the "unspeakable satisfaction" of rushing an aide to the French officer and asking if *he* needed reinforcements to capture redoubt nine, which was still resisting.

On October 17, as the allied cannons kept up their incessant pounding, Cornwallis asked for a truce to discuss surren-

Darley's sketch of American troops led by Alexander Hamilton storming the British outpost, redoubt ten.

der terms. Outnumbered almost two to one, with his ammunition running out and his casualties mounting, the British commander surrendered his army on the morning of October 19, 1781. Later that day, the defeated British troops marched out of the rubble of Yorktown in their dress uniforms. Passing between the Americans lining one side of the road and the French on the other, they refused to look at the Americans, turning their heads toward the French troops on their right. As they approached Lafayette's

Surrender at Yorktown. The British commander, General Cornwallis, pleading illness, failed to attend the surrender ceremony. From a painting by John Trumbull.

division, he ordered his drum major to strike up "Yankee Doodle," and with the pulse of drums and the squeal of fifes, that was the tune that accompanied the British soldiers as they made their way to an open field and gave up their arms.

Yorktown was the last major battle of the Revolutionary War. The British defeat was so devastating that even Lord North, the British prime minister, considered that battle the final blow. "Oh God," North exclaimed, pacing up and down, when he was informed that Cornwallis had surrendered. "Oh God. It is all over. It is all over."

Although skirmishes continued, both sides prepared for the diplomatic negotiations that resulted in the Treaty of Paris, signed on September 3, 1783, formally recognizing American independence.

By then, Lafayette was back in France.

The last page of the Treaty of Paris from the National Archives, featuring the seals and signatures of David Hartley, John Adams, Benjamin Franklin, and John Jay, signed on September 3, 1783. The treaty formally ended the Revolutionary War.

❧ Ten ❧

In Search of Liberty

When Lafayette returned to France in January 1782, seeking more aid for the Americans, Yorktown and his role in that decisive battle had become the talk of Paris. "The reception I have met from the nation at large, from the King and from my friends . . . surpassed my utmost ambition," he wrote to Washington.

Poems and pamphlets praising Lafayette were on sale at every Paris bookstall. Crowds followed his carriage through the streets, cheering and applauding. At the age of twenty-four, he was commissioned a general in the French army. And at a gala ball in Versailles's glittering Hall of Mirrors, he danced with Marie Antoinette by the light of five thousand candles. This time, he did not stumble.

Lafayette and Adrienne bought a home of their own, which became famous for its "American dinners," attended by Benjamin Franklin and other American dignitaries who were visiting or living in Paris. A portrait of Washington dominated the drawing room. Adrienne gave birth to another child, a daughter named Virginie in honor of Washington's home state. And Lafayette worked tirelessly to gain continuing French aid for his adopted country, the United States of America.

He returned to an America newly independent and at peace in the summer of 1784 for an emotional reunion with Washington and a triumphant farewell tour accompanied at

every stop by booming cannon salutes, parades, banquets, and speeches. Though he had just turned twenty-six, his receding hairline and expanding paunch added years to his appearance. "The Marquis has an old head upon young shoulders," one of his hosts observed.

At Mount Vernon, Lafayette embraced Washington for the first time in three years. "Our meeting was very tender and our satisfaction completely mutual," he wrote to Adrienne. In Massachusetts, Harvard University awarded the marquis an honorary Doctor of Laws degree, which he accepted in Latin. A county in Pennsylvania was named after him—the first of hundreds of American places and institutions to carry Lafayette's name. And at Lake Oneida in northern New York, he renewed his friendship with the Indian tribes of the Iroquois Confederacy, which was negotiating a new peace treaty with the United States.

To reach Lake Oneida, Lafayette and his party had to travel across the all-but-trackless wilderness during a bitter, late-autumn cold spell. After their carriages broke down, they rode the rest of the way on workhorses with blankets for saddles. The only member of the increasingly miserable group who remained in good spirits was Lafayette, "who appears to be proof against heat, cold, drought, moisture and the intemperance of the weather," one of the travelers recalled.

Lafayette's defense against the advancing cold was a heavy cloak he had brought to America packed in newspapers. In the dampness of the transatlantic crossing, the newspapers had become stuck to the thick cloth of the cloak, and since they served as insulation, he hadn't bothered to peel them off. One of his companions joked that watching Lafayette get dressed in the morning gave him a chance to catch up on the latest headlines from Europe.

Six years earlier, the Oneidas had adopted Lafayette into their tribe, and now they greeted him warmly. "Mr. de la Fayette has their confidence and their devotion to an extraordinary degree," the French ambassador noted in his diary. "Those who have seen him before have a great urge to see him again. They have communicated their enthusiasms to their friends, and they seem proud to wear around their necks some trinket that he once gave them."

He was welcomed just as warmly each time he met with his former comrades-in-arms. "My dear brother officers," he tearfully assured one group, "that I early enlisted with you in the cause of liberty shall be the pride and satisfaction of my life."

Americans in 1784 were debating and writing what would soon become the United States Constitution. Wherever he went, Lafayette spoke in favor of a strong central government for the newly united states, to avoid the rivalries and quarrels that so often resulted in wars among Europe's collection of independent nations. And nearly eighty years before Abraham Lincoln's Emancipation Proclamation, Lafayette urged his American friends to abolish the slave trade and free every slave. The world was looking to America, he told Congress, to "stand [as] a lesson to oppressors, an example to the oppressed, [and] a sanctuary for the rights of mankind."

When his farewell tour ended, Washington saw him off. He watched Lafayette's carriage disappear around a bend in the road as he left Mount Vernon to catch the ship that was waiting for him in New York. "I often asked myself," Washington wrote to his departed friend, "whether that was the last sight I ever should have of you? And though I wished to say no, my fears answered yes."

Lafayette had much to think about on the voyage home. He had sailed to America as a teenager in pursuit of military glory, and had learned what it is like to fight a war with an under-equipped force of part-time soldiers enduring every danger and privation for the cause of liberty. Tested in battle, bonded to his troops, he had proved his courage. In working for personal acclaim he had come to worship the ideals that would guide him for the rest of life.

"In striving for my own glory," he had told Adrienne, "I work for their happiness. . . . The welfare of America is intimately linked with the happiness of all mankind; she will become the respected and safe asylum of virtue, integrity, tolerance, equality, and a peaceful liberty."

Lafayette devoted the rest of his long life to seeking the same political liberties for his native land that he had helped win for America. He became a leading figure of the French Revolution, a bloody, chaotic affair that kept France in turmoil for decades. King Louis XVI and Marie Antoinette, among many others, lost their heads to the guillotine. As Lafayette unhappily discovered, the American Revolution was not easily transplanted to France.

Lafayette back in France in his uniform as commander of the French National Guard.

"Take care, young men," the Reverend Samuel Cooper of Boston had warned a group of French officers who were eager to return home and spread the word about the triumph of liberty. "Take care. . . . You carry home with you the seeds of liberty, but if you attempt to plant them in [France], you will face obstacles far more formidable than we did. We spilled a great deal of blood to win our liberty, but to establish it in the old world, you will shed it in torrents."

Americans had been well prepared for self-government by their colonial institutions. Public issues in America were discussed, debated, and argued over in town meetings, not decided in a royal chamber and dictated from above. The king of France was an absolute ruler; his word was law. At the time, French citizens had virtually no experience in self-government.

Lafayette called for an end to the king's absolute rule. He urged the establishment of a constitutional monarchy that would force the king to share his power with the people and that would guarantee fundamental rights to every citizen. His efforts to spread the gospel of political liberty were seen as a direct challenge to the king's power and a threat to all European monarchs. At the same time, as head of the French National Guard, he was viewed as an enemy by the revolutionary factions that had seized power in France, and he was punished severely. Accused of treason, he lost his fortune and his freedom.

In 1792, to avoid certain execution on the guillotine, Lafayette gave himself up to France's enemies and spent the next five years in a succession of dank dungeon cells, first in Prussia and later in Austria, at times shackled in solitary confinement. And while he was imprisoned, members of his family suffered. His wife's sister, mother, and elderly grandmother, denounced as "enemies of the state," were delivered to the guillotine. Adrienne herself spent sixteen months in a Paris prison before being freed with the help of the American envoys Gouverneur Morris and future president James Monroe. Eventually, Adrienne and her daughters were allowed to join Lafayette at Olmutz, a forbidding prison in Austria, where, amid mounting worldwide protests at their treatment, they became known as "the Prisoners of Olmutz."

Released in 1797, Lafayette and his family went into exile in Denmark. Three years later he was permitted to return to France, where he settled on a farm called La Grange, which his wife had inherited from her mother.

The Prisoners of Olmutz. Lafayette's wife, Adrienne, and his two daughters joined him in prison from 1795–1797.

Château de La Grange, Lafayette's home after he returned to France from prison and exile.

73

With his citizenship restored, Lafayette again became an influential voice in French politics. He resumed his battle for French political freedoms and his outspoken support for liberation movements throughout the world. His Declaration of the Rights of Man and of the Citizen—which had been approved by the National Assembly of France in 1789—declared that "all men are born free and equal in rights" and "all citizens have freedom of thought, speech, writing, printing, and publishing." In Lafayette's lifetime, however, his hopes for a truly democratic France were never realized. Even so, he never lost his faith in the ultimate triumph of liberty. The concept of liberty, he said as an old man, "inflames me today as it did at nineteen."

In 1824, when Lafayette was sixty-seven years old, the United States Congress invited him to revisit the nation he had helped create, "to see for himself the fruit borne on the tree of liberty." As the nation's guest he toured each of the twenty-four states, and wherever he went, from Boston to New Orleans to Fayetteville, the North Carolina city named after him, he was greeted by enthusiastic crowds of admiring Americans who had turned out to see the last surviving general of the Revolutionary War and to hear him speak. When one eager well-wisher congratulated him on his ability to speak to Americans in their own language, Lafayette replied: "And why would I not speak English? I am an American, after all—just returned from a long visit to Europe."

This time his tour lasted thirteen months. Afterward he sailed back to France aboard an American ship named the *Brandywine* in his honor. The *Brandywine* was loaded down with tons of gifts and souvenirs that Lafayette had collected along the way, including several sacks filled with soil from Bunker Hill and from the battlefield at Brandywine Creek, where he had shed his blood for America. When he died in 1834, he was buried, as he wished, in that American soil at a small cemetery on the outskirts of Paris.

Eighty-three years later, in 1917, when the American Expeditionary Forces came to France's aid during World War I, Lafayette's name was still synonymous with French-American friendship. The first American troops to arrive in France made a pilgrimage to Lafayette's burial place. In a stirring tribute to the young Frenchman's heroic service to America, U.S. Colonel Charles E. Stanton stood before the grave, saluted, and announced: "Lafayette, we are here."

Senior statesman Lafayette at seventy-five in his garden at Château de La Grange. From a painting by Louise Adeone Joubert.

Lafayette leading troops into battle.

Time Line

1757: Gilbert du Motier de Lafayette is born at his family's château in Chavaniac, France.

1759: Father is killed by a British cannonball at the Battle of Minden in the Seven Years' War. Gilbert inherits the family titles.

1768: Moves to Paris to live with his mother.

1770: Mother dies. Becomes a ward of his great-grandfather, the comte de la Rivière.

1771: Enrolls in the king's elite corps, the Black Musketeers.

1774: Marries Marie-Adrienne-Françoise de Noailles. Commissioned a lieutenant in the Noailles Dragoons, a cavalry regiment under the hereditary patronage of his wife's family.

1775: Promoted to captain. Soon afterward placed on indefinite leave.

1776: The American Revolutionary War breaks out. Lafayette volunteers to join the Continental army and is promised a major general's commission.

1777: Sails to America, joins Washington's staff, and is wounded at the Battle of Brandywine on September 11. Washington leads his troops to winter quarters at Valley Forge, arriving December 19.

1778: Commands the ill-fated Canadian expedition. Meets with tribal members of the Iroquois Confederacy. Word of the alliance with France reaches Valley Forge on May 1. Battles of Barren Hill, May 20, and Monmouth Courthouse, June 28.

1779: Sails back to France. Wins French support for the American cause.

1780: Returns to America on April 27. French fleet and army arrive in Newport, Rhode Island.

1781: Commanding a small mobile force, Lafayette traps General Cornwallis on Virginia's Yorktown peninsula. The combined American and French forces win the Battle of Yorktown, and the British surrender on October 19.

1782: Arrives in France to honors and public acclaim.

1783: The Treaty of Paris officially ends the Revolutionary War on September 3. Britain recognizes American independence.

1784: Returns to the United States for a farewell tour. Visits Washington for the last time.

1786: In France, calls for sweeping political and economic reforms under a constitutional monarchy.

1789: Lafayette's Declaration of the Rights of Man and of the Citizen is approved by the French National Assembly. The storming of the Bastille prison in Paris on July 14 marks the beginning of the French Revolution. Lafayette organizes the National Guard.

1792: Accused of treason, flees France, and is imprisoned by the king of Prussia.

1794: Lafayette's wife is imprisoned in Paris. Her sister, mother, and grandmother are among the thousands of people guillotined.

1795: Adrienne and her daughters join Lafayette in prison at Olmutz, Austria.

1797: American officials help win the release of the Lafayettes. They return to France in 1799 and retire to Château de La Grange.

1814: Resuming his political career, Lafayette is elected to the French National Assembly.

1824: Returns to the United States for a thirteen-month triumphal tour.

1834: Dies in Paris on May 20.

Source Notes

The following notes refer to the sources of quoted material. Each citation includes the first and last words or phrases of the quotation and the source. Unless otherwise noted, all references are to works cited in the Selected Bibliography.

Abbreviations used:

Bobrick—Benson Bobrick, *Angel in the Whirlwind*
Buckman—Peter Buckman, *Lafayette*
Gaines—James R. Gaines, *For Liberty and Glory*
Gottschalk I—Louis Gottschalk, *Lafayette Comes to America*
Gottschalk II—Louis Gottschalk, *Lafayette Joins the American Army*
Idzerda I & II—Stanley J. Idzerda, *Lafayette in the Age of the American Revolution,* vols. I & II
Liberty—Thomas Fleming, *Liberty! The American Revolution*
Rebels—George E. Scheer and Hugh E. Rankin, *Rebels and Redcoats*
Scheer—George E. Scheer, *Yankee Doodle Boy*
'76—Henry Steele Commager and Richard B. Morris, *The Spirit of Seventy-Six*
Unger—Harlow Giles Unger, *Lafayette*

Page

ONE: THE MYSTERIOUS STANGER
1 "the gentleman . . . first floor": Gottschalk I, p. 93
3 "you will . . . miss me": Idzerda I, pp. 28–29

TWO: THE LITTLE LORD OF CHAVANIAC
6 "Beast of Gévaudan": Buckman, p. 12
"My heart . . . very exciting": Idzerda I, p. 6
10 "Lafayette always . . . spoke little": Unger, p. 14
"My awkward . . . court": Gaines, p. 36; Idzerda I, p. 3
11 "Everyone knows . . . wit": Gaines, p. 37
12 "Yes . . . green coat": Gottschalk I, p. 48

Page

THREE: WHY NOT?
14 "When I first . . . revolutionaries": Gaines, p. 37; Idzerda I, p.7
15 "All men . . . of the laws": Voltaire (François Marie Arouet), *Essay on Manners*, 1756
16 "well-nigh . . . to America": Gottschalk I, p. 70
"I watched . . . unnecessarily": Gaines, p. 53
17 "Good . . . care of it!": Gottschalk I, p. 74
18 "till he can go. . . . major general": Unger, p. 22; Idzerda I, p. 17
"with plenty . . . severity": Gottschalk I, p. 79
19 "Before this . . . danger": Idzerda I, p. 8
Cur non? (Why not?): Gottschalk I, p. 85

FOUR: ESCAPE FROM FRANCE
22 "Do not . . . to you": Idzerda I, p. 32
"I was . . . everybody": Unger, p. 27
23 "You are . . . further orders": Idzerda I, p. 9
"If he . . . to do": Unger, p. 26
24 "I have just . . . men": Unger, p. 26
25 "so noble an enterprise": Gottschalk I, p. 119
26 "Don't worry . . . enterprise": Gaines, p. 56; Idzerda I, p. 51
"It's undoubtedly . . . blame him": Gottschalk I, p. 104
"I do not . . . about it": Gottschalk I, p. 125
"has occasioned . . . in France": Gottschalk I, p. 130
27 "blow up": Idzerda I, p. 10
"[H]aving to choose . . . forgiven me": Idzerda I, pp. 56–57
"One day . . . same thing": Idzerda I, pp. 56–57

FIVE: "HERE TO LEARN"
29 "I retired . . . pursuers": Unger, p. 32
30 "we arrived . . . celebrations": Unger, p. 34; Idzerda I, p. 73
"By the fourth . . . dysentery": Idzerda I, p. 76

30 "The farther . . . people": Gottschalk II, p. 11

"no campaign . . . Charleston": Idzerda I, p. 76

31 "It seems . . . plenty of them": Unger, p. 36; Idzerda I, p. 77

"We did not . . . about it": Idzerda I, p. 77

32 "After the sacrifices . . . volunteer": Idzerda I, p. 11

32–33 "Whereas . . . United States": Idzerda I, p.88

33 "Although [Washington] . . . deportment": Gaines, p. 68

"eleven thousand men . . . French army": Idzerda I, p. 91

"I am here . . . teach": Idzerda I, p. 91

34 "By the time . . . thin wood": Unger, pp. 43–44

"Cannons roaring . . . as this": Gaines, p. 74

35 "a steady . . . wall to wall": Gaines, p. 74

36 "The whole army . . . escape": '76, p. 614

"Sir . . . sustained": '76, p. 616–617

"Treat him . . . son": Bobrick, p. 296

SIX: WINTER AT VALLEY FORGE

38 "Consider . . . myself": Gottschalk II, pp. 55–56

"He is . . . enthusiasm": Gottschalk II, p. 63, p. 80

"The Marquis . . . danger": Gottschalk II, p. 82

39 "He is more . . . consequences": Gottschalk II, p. 85

"It is . . . army": Gottschalk II, p. 85

"By skillfully . . . quarters": Idzerda I, p. 169

40 "The unfortunate . . . renewed": Unger, p. 58; Idzerda I, p. 170

41 "military family": Harlow Giles Unger, *The Unexpected George Washington: His Private Life* (Hoboken, NJ: John Wiley & Sons, 2006), p. 119

"The better . . . him": Bobrick, p. 296

"Our general . . . without him": Idzerda I, p. 192

"We are not . . . committed to it": Unger, p. 56; Idzerda I, p. 193

42 "The idea . . . upon it": Unger, p. 65; Idzerda I, p. 275

"I have consulted . . . operation": Idzerda I, p. 296

"My situation . . . blunders": Idzerda I, p. 296

"Why am I . . . themselves?": Idzerda I, p. 299

"It will be . . . [invasion]": Idzerda I, p. 342

43–44 "Five hundred . . . power": Unger, p. 68

45 "The very . . . envied him": Unger, p. 51

46 "Very happy . . . satisfaction": Secret War, p. 248

SEVEN: THE BATTLES OF BARREN HILL AND MONMOUTH COURTHOUSE

47 "stout-looking . . . neat": Scheer, p. 83

48 "We were told . . . there": Scheer, pp. 83–84

"had invited . . . night": Unger, p. 76; Idzerda II, p. 7

50 "The enemy . . . good order": Scheer, pp. 84–85

"snare . . . manner": Buckman, p. 73

"finished or unfinished": James Thomas Flexner, *Washington: The Indispensible Man* (Boston: Little, Brown, 1969, 1973, 1974), p. 119

51 "or otherwise annoy the enemy": Gaines, p. 114

"The young Frenchman . . . distinguish himself": Gaines, p. 114

52 "all along . . . superb a man": Rebels, p. 331

EIGHT: HERO OF TWO WORLDS

54 "We recommend . . . war": Idzerda II, p. 194

55 "My joy . . . world": Unger, p. 95

56 "Love . . . American cause": Idzerda II, p. 292

"I had left . . . idol": Unger, p. 94

"The hero of two worlds": Gaines, p. 135

"whose success . . . doubt": Unger, p. 98

"not only . . . complex": Buckman, p. 83

57 "I don't . . . Genl. Washington": Unger, p. 107

"I ardently wish . . . forever": Idzerda II, pp. 277–281

"kept you . . . can impair": Idzerda II, p. 314

NINE: "THE BOY CANNOT ESCAPE ME"

59 "Here I am . . . young soldier": Unger, p. 111

60 "The confidence . . . riches": Gaines, p. 141

61 "The boy . . . Richmond": Buckman, p. 103; Bobrick, p. 442; Rebels, p. 470

"of a general defeat . . . beaten": Rebels, p. 470

62 "Were I . . . too far": Rebels, p. 470

63 "Should a French . . . be ours": Unger, p. 152

64 "do all . . . by land": '76, p. 1217

64–65 "The temptation . . . blood": Unger, p. 155

65 "unspeakable satisfaction": Liberty, p. 330

67 "Oh God . . . all over": Liberty, p. 336

TEN: IN SEARCH OF LIBERTY

68 "The reception . . . ambition": Gaines, p. 179

"American dinners": Gaines, p. 180

69 "The Marquis . . . shoulders": Unger, p.193

"Our meeting . . . mutual": Gaines, p. 198

70 "who appears . . . weather": Gaines, p. 203

"Mr. de la Fayette . . . gave them": Unger, p. 197

"My dear . . . my life": Unger, p. 194

71 "stand [as] a lesson . . . mankind": Gaines, p. 208

"I often . . . answered yes": Buckman, p. 118

71 "In striving . . . peaceful liberty": Idzerda I, pp. 58–59

72 "Take care . . . torrents": Gaines, p. 166

73 "enemies of the state": Gaines, p. 379

"the Prisoners of Olmutz": Gaines, p. 393

74 "all men . . . publishing": Gaines, p. 279

"inflames . . . at nineteen": Gaines, p. 397

"to see . . . liberty": Gaines, p. 439

75 "And why . . . Europe": Unger, p. 355

"Lafayette, we are here": Unger, p. 380

Selected Bibliography

The two American scholars whose work on Lafayette is considered definitive are Louis Gottschalk of the University of Chicago and Stanley J. Idzerda of Cornell University. Gottschalk's life's work stands today as the most comprehensive biography of Lafayette in English; he died before it could be finished. The sixth volume ends in July 1790, at the first anniversary of the fall of the Bastille, with Lafayette at the height of his power and popularity. First published in 1935, Gottschalk's massive study remains an indispensable and highly readable source. My account draws mainly on the first two volumes: *Lafayette Comes to America* and *Lafayette Joins the American Army* (Chicago: University of Chicago Press, 1935 and 1937).

Idzerda, in collaboration with others, was editor of the five-volume *Lafayette in the Age of the American Revolution: Selected Letters and Papers, 1776-1790* (Ithaca: Cornell University Press, 1977, 1979, 1980, 1981, 1983). These volumes include selections from Lafayette's personal memoirs and exchanges of letters with members of his family and with notable political figures of the era; those written in French appear both in the original and in translation.

Recent biographies include Harlow Giles Unger's *Lafayette* (Hoboken, New Jersey: John Wiley and Sons, 2002), an admiring account that presents Lafayette as an "gallant knight" and impassioned advocate of American republican and constitutional ideals; James R. Gaines's *For Liberty and Glory: Washington, Lafayette and Their Revolution* (New York: W. W. Norton, 2007), a scholarly dual biography that analyzes the friendship between Washington and Lafayette and the inseparable links between the American and French revolutions; and Peter Buchanan's *Lafayette: A Biography* (New York & London: Paddington Press, 1977), a relatively concise, straightforward account.

David A. Clary's *Adopted Son: Washington, Lafayette, and the Friendship that Saved the Union* (New York: Bantam, 2008) focuses, as the title suggests, on the relationship between Washington and Lafayette and argues that their bond was a key to the success of the American Revolution. Jason Lane's *General and Madame de Lafayette: Partners in Liberty's Cause in the American and French Revolutions* (Lanham, Maryland: Taylor Trade Publishing, 2003) deals with Lafayette's relationship with his devoted wife, Adrienne, who died at fifty due to an illness contracted at the Austrian prison where she elected to join her incarcerated husband.

Henry Steele Commager and Richard B. Morris's *The Spirit of Seventy-Six: The Story of the American Revolution as Told by Participants* (New York: Harper & Row, 1967) and George E. Scheer and Hugh E. Rankin's *Rebels and Redcoats: The American Revolution Through the Eyes of Those Who Fought and Lived It* (New York: World Publishing Company, 1957) are essential collections of writings and documents from the revolutionary era. Scheer also edited *Yankee Doodle Boy: A Young Soldier's Adventures in the American Revolution Told by Himself* (New York: Holiday House, 1995), Joseph Plumb Martin's autobiographical account of his wartime experiences, first published in 1830.

Among many noteworthy books on the American Revolution, I found the following particularly helpful: Benson Bobrick's *Angel in the Whirlwind: The Triumph of the American Revolution* (New York: Simon & Schuster, 1997); John Buchanan's *The Road to Valley Forge: How Washington Built the Army that Won the Revolution* (Hoboken, NJ: John Wiley & Sons, 2004); Thomas Fleming's *Washington's Secret War: The Hidden History of Valley Forge* (New York: HarperCollins, 2005); and Fleming's *Liberty! The American Revolution* (New York: Viking, 1997).

Books for young readers include Jean Fritz's *Why Not Lafayette?* (New York: G. P. Putnam's, 1999) and Richard Ferrie's *The World Turned Upside Down: George Washington and the Battle of Yorktown* (New York: Holiday House, 1999).

Picture Credits

Centre historique des Archives nationales, Musée de l'histoire de France: 74

Division of Rare and Manuscript Collections, Cornell University Library: 5, 8, 73 (top)

Emmet Collection, Miriam and Ira D. Wallach Division of Art, Prints and Photographs, The New York Public Library, Astor, Lenox and Tilden Foundations: 21 (right), 28, 35, 61

Getty Images: 3

Grafton, John. *The American Revolution: A Picture Sourcebook.* New York: Dover Publications, 1975: 14, 31, 33, 45 (top), 62 (top and bottom), 64, 65

Library of Congress: 49, 60, 69, 72, 76

Marquis de Lafayette Collections, Manuscript Inventory Series I, Hubbard Collection, Lafayette College: 41 (bottom)

Marquis de Lafayette Manuscript Collection, Special Collections and College Archives, David Skillman Library, Lafayette College: 9, 73 (bottom)

Mary Evans Picture Library: 11, 19, 23, 24, 54 (top)

The Monmouth County Historical Association, Freehold, New Jersey. "Washington at the Battle of Monmouth," Emanuel Leutze (1816–1868), oil on canvas, dated 1857, gift of the descendants of David Leavitt, 1937: 51

Musée de l'Armée, Dist. Réunion de Musées Nationaux /Art Resource, New York: 75

National Park Service, Museum Management Program and Independence National Historical Park, Portrait of Johann de Kalb by Charles Willson Peale, INDE 14084, http://www.nps.gov/history/museum/exhibits/revwar/image_gal/indeimg/dekalb.html: 21 (left)

National Park Service, Museum Management Program and Independence National Historical Park, Portrait of Nathanael Greene by Charles Willson Peale, INDE 14055, http://www.nps.gov/history/museum/exhibits/revwar/image_gal/indeimg/greene.html: 38

Pennsylvania Capitol Preservation Committee and Brian Hunt: 45 (bottom)

Picture Collection, The New York Public Library, Astor, Lenox and Tilden Foundations: 37, 40, 43, 48

Print Collection, Miriam and Ira D. Wallach Division of Art, Prints and Photographs, The New York Public Library, Astor, Lenox and Tilden Foundations: 17, 47 (both)

Public Domain: 2, 6, 10 (both), 15, 32, 41 (top right), 41 (top left), 54 (bottom), 55, 57, 58, 66

Réunion des Musées Nationaux / Art Resource, New York: iv, 13, 27

Scala /Art Resource: viii

Treaty of Paris, 1783; International Treaties and Related Records, 1778–1974; General Records of the United States Government, Record Group 11; National Archives: 67

Index